D1064833

# The Reservation Blackfeet, 1882–1945

## A Photographic History of Cultural Survival

*"The Three Chiefs"*

# The Reservation Blackfeet, 1882–1945

## A Photographic History of Cultural Survival

WILLIAM E. FARR *With a Foreword by James Welch*

UNIVERSITY OF WASHINGTON PRESS *Seattle & London*

*For my wife Marianne, with whom
I learn the important things.*

This book was published with the support of the Johnson-O'Malley Committee,
School District #9, Browning, Montana.

Library of Congress Cataloging in Publication Data

Farr, William E., 1938–
    The reservation Blackfeet, 1882–1945

    Bibliography: p.
    Includes index.
        1. Siksika Indians — History.   2. Blackfeet Indian
Reservation (Mont.) — History.   3. Indians of North
America — Montana — History.   I. Title.
E99.S54F37   1984          978.6′00497          83–47975
ISBN 0–295–96040–X

*Photo: page i*

## Jack Big Moon, sentinel at Sun Dance encampment, ca. 1899

An inverted U painted on the horse indicates a raiding expedition undertaken. *Photo by
Walter McClintock; courtesy of Glacier National Park Archives*

# Contents

Foreword by James Welch  vii

Preface  ix

Acknowledgments  xix

The End of the Buffalo Days  3

After the Buffalo: *Old Agency on Badger Creek*  9

Social Management: *Implanting Reservation Institutions*  38

The Sun Dance: *Tradition as Inspiration*  66

Getting By: *The Economics of Survival*  97

A Diminished Way of Life: *Changes in Tradition*  138

Blackfeet in a Modern World: *The Past Remains*  169

"So That's What It Was Like": *The Blackfeet and Their Photographers*  187

Epilogue  202

Select Bibliography  204

Index  206

*Woman pitching a tepee*

Photo by Walter McClintock; courtesy of Glacier National Park Archives

# Foreword

I REMEMBER standing beside my father on a hot summer day on a plain southwest
of Browning, near the Two Medicine River. I was standing beside my father and
we were standing in the middle of an encampment of traditional painted tepees.
There were many straight-sided canvas tents around the perimeter of the camp.
Pickups and beaten cars glinted harshly beneath a roaring sun. Dogs barked and horses
grunted and whickered and somewhere not far off a child cried. Perhaps the child was
my young brother, held high in my mother's arms, squirming to see over the headdresses
and roaches of the people in front of us. The air smelled of smoky buckskin and sagebrush
and the burning sweetgrass. The people grew silent and attentive. We were watching a
tepee not far to the west of the big half-finished medicine lodge. Behind me I heard
the whirr of a home movie camera. I was a little frightened, I remember.

Then the lodge flap was lifted away and the first head appeared. My father nudged
me. One by one they emerged, these holy Blackfeet. The master of ceremonies, large
and far-seeing, led the procession. Behind him slowly strode the medicine woman's
husband, his body blackened by charcoal, symbols of moon and sun on chest and back,
his face lined with sun dogs. Next came the previous year's sacred vow woman, who
had transferred the paraphernalia in an elaborate ceremony within the lodge. Then came
the medicine woman with her helpers behind her. She wore an elkskin dress, an elkskin
cape, and a headdress made of buffalo hide, weasel skins, and feathers. Attached to the
front was a doll stuffed with tobacco seeds and human hair. It was a sacred headdress.
In her arms she held a sacred digging stick. Two of her assistants walked close beside
her, holding those arms, for she was weak and frail from her fast. In my youthful distortion
(I was nine at the time), I imagined her to be ninety years old, but now I suspect she
was closer to fifty. Her helpers carried in their parfleches the sacred tongues, once buffalo,
now beef or elk — I don't remember — to be distributed to the people. As they made
their way to the medicine lodge, a voice, high and distant, sang to the sun and it entered
my bones and I was Blackfeet and changed forever. I remember.

Thirty-four years later the image of that Sun Dance procession is still with me, and
in my novels and poems I have tried to maintain the spirit of that moment. It is difficult
these days, when one is standing on the main street in Browning, a chilly March wind
banging against the shabby buildings and one's own face, to remember that people,

whoever they are, dwell not only upon the land, but also within the land, and within the sky, the trees, the mountains and the plains.

The Blackfeet are such a people, and *The Reservation Blackfeet* tells their story powerfully and well. The photographs provide a fascinating, moving montage of a people trying to adapt to a new way of life and of a government's often misguided attempts to re-create a people consistent with its notion of a homogenous America. As the photographs witness, many of the Blackfeet went along with the program, learning to farm, to read, to make baskets. Others resisted, not out of an innate hostility toward things white, but because they could foresee the day when white culture would replace their own.

William E. Farr's text provides the photographs not only with a historical context but with an illumination that only the best writing can. It is clear from his text that this book is a labor of love, of sympathy, of outrage — and of truth.

But it is the photographs themselves that tell the story. Study them. Look into the faces. Study the detail in the traditional dress, the paintings on the lodges, the attitudes of the horses. Watch the children play, the women work or "visit" in their new-fangled cotton dresses, and the men play "stick game" with their sleeves rolled up. Then look into the faces. A hundred years after the Starvation Winter of 1883–84 their children can look upon them with pride.

*James Welch*

# Preface

THIS PHOTOGRAPHIC HISTORY of the Blackfeet and their reservation had its genesis in conversations with Gary Schmautz, a friend who teaches history at Browning High School. I had developed an interest in historical photographs and had put together an exhibit that traveled the small, local museums of Montana. Gary asked me if I thought old photographs might be one way to interest Blackfeet students in their own history. He went on to say that although now, more then ever, Indian young people wanted their past to speak to them, it did not seem to be doing so through books. I too had encountered this situation. Young people searching to discover their past found the written word an obstacle rather than a welcome avenue. It took too much time to read, too much effort for too little return. Instead they wanted to experience, quickly and visually, and this they could do with historical photographs. If old photographs allowed for an enchanted entry into the past elsewhere, and I was convinced they did, why not on an Indian reservation?

Gary and I agreed to see if together we could uncover enough images to construct a visual history of the reservation Blackfeet. It was as if we set out to design a twentieth-century "winter count" that would continue, in a more elaborate fashion, the earlier Blackfeet attempts at reckoning time and recording outstanding individual and tribal events. Like other Plains Indians, the Piegan "counted" by keeping a kind of pictorial calendar, either drawing a chronology of events on hides or, more frequently, anchoring in memory an event to a particular winter. We too wanted to visualize tribal history — and we too wanted to compile slices of time remembered but ours, however, had been seldom painted on skin or anywhere else. Was such a photographic "winter count," a landscape of mechanical "picture writing," possible? We were not sure.

Teaching on the reservation, Gary had also uncovered a haunting, vital question that underlay so many glances, so many actions and decisions: how much could Indian people change and yet remain essentially Indian? Phrased in its crudest and most obvious form, if you don't look like a stereotype Indian, can you be one? This conflict between change and cultural survival surfaced as the central theme of this photographic history. The fact that the Blackfeet had changed was certainly documented in the photographs taken between 1882 and 1945. If there was a single overwhelming reality on the reservation in that period it was change — irrepressible and uncontainable. Answers to the question of cultural survival, however, are more elusive and more personal. Could photographs

*Shortie White Grass, head of the Buffalo Dung band, 1899*

White Grass, pictured here with an unidentified man, was not only a medicine man but had been a daring warrior who had taken part in many successful raids during the intertribal war period prior to the 1880s. White Grass's war exploits were documented by means of picture-writing on a hide by a Piegan artist named Sharp. Later White Grass himself drew something of his war record for the Great Northern Railroad about 1919. *Photo by Walter McClintock; courtesy of Glacier National Park Archives*

give clues about what had been gained and what had been salvaged and what had been lost? We thought so.

After the 1880s the Blackfeet possessed a new document, the photograph, to supplement the Indian oral tradition and the white written one. The camera recorded something of the Blackfeet's transformation. A wealth of photographs now registered people's faces — a crooked smile, narrow-eyed defiance, wide-eyed acceptance. There was nuance, tone, and the subtle distinctions that left people and situations discrete. History spoke with a new and clearer voice.

Once we began looking, in the spring of 1978, we encountered old photographs everywhere — in family albums, on kitchen walls next to the wood stove, nestled away in dresser drawers under the socks, and in little libraries in little towns surrounded by trees. In fact, we stumbled into a sprawling historical world that was large, astonishingly accessible, and yet surprisingly neglected. Here were windowpanes that looked out on the past as if onto your neighbor's backyard. We, and others, had found earlier reservation reality so terribly difficult to imagine, and then, with these fixed, rectangular glimpses, it was suddenly there.

The photographs depicted Sun Dance encampments, sham battles, women talking, a sewing machine outside a cotton duck tepee, braids against a suit coat. It was a new world with different rhythms and habits. It was also an uncertain one. This alluring pictorial world confirmed and denied the stereotype images of Indians, and it triggered in our imaginations an army of situations that had somehow escaped the sight of the photographer. Caught in the tide of what had been, these real and imagined photos verified a Blackfeet history that we had heard or read about but could not see.

Particularly interesting was the tremendous weight of historical detail — the photos distinguished and identified particular people, specific times, and recognizable places. Instead of filtering out the meaningful detail, as textbook generalizations so often do, these backward glimpses piled one upon another, composing in the process a layered reality one almost could touch. It was not so much that the old photographs explained the past; written accounts did that. Rather, they pictured it. Stripping away the heavy curtain of years, the photographs revealed the bright and surprising different world that had been lost.

Slowly we gathered a treasury of images that invited continual speculation. It grew in bits and pieces — a negative here, a dog-eared scrap of a loved one there. Sometimes a mother would bring in a whole album; sometimes a hand released a single sparkling print, without creases or cracks. Now, five years later in 1983, that initial treasury has grown to include several hundred items.

People both on and off the reservation and in and out of Montana have contributed. Sadly, we found more photographs off the Blackfeet Reservation than on it; more resided in white hands than in red. We had not expected that. Perhaps we should have. After all, few Indian people during the early years of the reservation had either the leisure, the economic means or the inclination to indulge in photography. Moreover, while white settlers may have wanted to note their novel presence and achievement on the Montana

*Jack Big Moon in capote made of a Hudson's Bay blanket, searching for game with a brass telescope*

*Photo courtesy of Southwest Museum*

prairies by means of the camera, Indian people had preferred to rely instead upon a rich oral tradition to record the presence and pace of their lives.

After about 1910, however, photographs became increasingly popular with individual Indian families; portraits of loved ones — grandmothers, children, aunts, and uncles — carefully were protected. By the 1930s and 1940s, snapshot albums and Kodak Brownie cameras were almost as common on the reservation as beyond its boundaries. Unfortunately, many of these family photographs and albums were lost in the tremendous flood of 1964, when so many Indian homes located along the creeks and rivers east of the Rocky Mountains were swept away.

In spite of these difficulties, by scouring libraries, by chasing leads through the telephone, through letters, and through personal contacts, we gradually amassed a body of materials. By relying upon the generosity, the interest, and the trust of many, many people we pieced together a picture of the reservation that was more revealing, more vibrant with life and personality than much of the previous work dealing with the Blackfeet.

Interesting discoveries cropped up. In the first place, the past that the photographs described was infinitely more complicated and specialized than we had thought. Secondly, the photographs showed the world of the reservation honestly, without distorting the recorded reality through the prism of language or culture.

The photographers usually were white, and they certainly wished to tell stories with their pictures. Yet, more often than not, their stories only tangentially addressed the changes the Blackfeet were experiencing. Those changes appear in the backgrounds or beside the subjects of the photographs. As the shutter on the camera clicked, the neutral lens, closely, objectively, registered life in a frame that was neither white nor red — it just was.

This mechanical aspect of the photograph, the camera as an impartial witness, has relaxed many concerns Indian people traditionally have entertained concerning other forms of historical documentation. Original white bias now could be filtered through Blackfeet eyes or a different generational interest. And gradually that interest could be focused on what the photographs said about the daily life and interests of Indian people. In this manner historical photographs could become another language, supplementing the oral tradition, to tell the Blackfeet who they had been.

Young Blackfeet in Browning High School found the photographs of their reservation fascinating. We scattered large, 16-by-20 prints on long library tables, urged young people to thumb through print files, and copied photographs from their grandmothers' albums. Students who said that they hated written history and did not want to read books would lean over to "read" photographs. Other students asked questions or commented on a situation that they saw in an old frame. They were intrigued and excited about what they saw, and in that excitement they seemed to find themselves standing in a Blackfeet tradition that now had gained greater meaning.

Most of our images we acquired by copying original photographs people sent us, or brought to us at Browning High School, or dropped off when they were in Missoula, Montana. This method of reproducing via copy negatives held a number of advantages.

*Blackfeet camp, ca. 1900*

*Photo by T. J. Hileman; courtesy of Sherburne Collection, UM Archives*

Especially, it meant that individuals and institutions would not have to give away their prized possessions — prized because they were family mementos, private parts of lives, or because they had a collector's value on the antique market.

There were, naturally, disadvantages as well. Copying original photographs costs a great deal of money. We applied to the Blackfeet's Johnson-O'Malley Committee for necessary funding. This committee, composed of Blackfeet parents and teachers, disburses federal monies authorized by the Johnson-O'Malley Act to various projects that further the education of Indian young people on the reservation. Our goal of using the historical photos to help preserve the Blackfeet cultural heritage and to render that heritage accessible found immediate support among committee members. The JOM Committee funded "Blackfeet Images," as we titled our effort, year after year, allowing us to develop the body of materials from which this book was distilled.

Once the photographs were all copied, we faced the fascinating if difficult task of identifying the people in them. We searched through the major and lesser-known works on the Blackfeet: the obscure C. C. Uhlenbeck, John Ewers's insightful works, and those issues of *Masterkey* that pertained. It was slow detective work matching names to faces and dates to events. Another method, of course, was to seek out tribal elders. Slowly, unknown faces became individuals.

For images which resisted divulging their identities, we submitted copy prints to a cultural committee of elders. They conducted their sessions in the Blackfeet tongue, pointing, remembering, arguing, and nearly always reached consensus. Whenever possible they tried to assign dates, places, and anecdotes to the pictures. As these elders pored over the little pieces of shiny paper, passing them around, there were sucked breaths of surprise, delighted cries of recognition, and sometimes a shrug when there was no recognition and a shuffle to the next photograph. There was a sense that those orphaned, unidentifiable photos were registering some break in tribal continuity or some past family loss. No one remembered.

However, Tom Many Guns reacted differently. He did not want to enter that special relationship when a subject encounters his old past in a photograph. One July afternoon we paid a call on Mr. Many Guns. A large, proud man, well over six feet four, Tom was absentmindedly watching a TV soap opera in his great-nephew's small, prefab house when we knocked on the door. He sat watching and waiting — to go downtown, to go to Canada to visit kinfolk, to sit in the sun on the bench in front of the Browning movie house.

We started to select photographs from the three file boxes. With no apparent interest he looked at the first few 8-by-10 photos. I did not know what was going through his mind. Just go slow, I thought. No need to hurry. Then I handed him an 8-by-10 taken fifty years before of himself and his first wife at the Browning Station on the way to Hollywood to make a movie. His eyes riveted on it and he reached for more, ignoring my questions. He called out to his shirtless nephew in "Indian" — there was shoulder in that voice. Reluctantly the nephew left the room and returned with a portable tape machine and Tom punched the play button with a thick finger. Drumming and keening

*On the move, ca. 1899*

*Photo by Walter McClintock; courtesy of Glacier National Park Archives*

song filled the room. For the next hour he peered, inspected, devoured, and reached for one photograph after another. He did not identify a single one. He did not say another word. Finally, he put his hands to his knees, slowly stood up, and left the room. He did not return.

The photographs that Tom Many Guns looked at but did not want, the same ones that the "Cultural Committee" had been over, often lacked clarity, artistic merit, or fine tonal quality. Lighting had been a problem in some; careless treatment had made others difficult to use. A few photographs had coffee rings; many more were wrinkled with floodwaters, torn from albums, or simply soiled with too much handling. Unfortunately, many negatives and prints appeared without comment, names, dates, or places. Now the distance is too great. Contemporaries have died, their children do not remember, and tribal elders like Many Guns cannot always bridge the gap with their memory even if they want to. Only the images remain.

As revealing as photographs are, anyone preparing a photographic history of the Blackfeet must recognize certain limitations. One is that no one attempted systematically to photograph reservation life. There had been in the nineteenth century sporadic attempts by a great variety of painters and later photographers to record an Indian past particularly after the Romantic movement goaded Americans into thinking about what was "passing away." This impulse to fix in time before it was too late convinced army personnel, boundary commissioners, surveyors, reservation doctors, and others to document in the easiest way — to photograph. There was no concentrated, systematic approach, however, to document a culture in transition, to rescue it from obscurity. Instead, numerous individuals worked alone and randomly. Some attempted to sell images of warriors to an Eastern public, others preserved for posterity, still others wanted to verify only themselves. Whatever the need to record, these tourists, government employees, and merchants stitched together a crazy quilt of images that is marked by jumps, gaps, and unexplained absences.

Further, some critical aspects of reservation life could not be photographed, either directly or even accidentally: the pungent smell of drifting wood smoke, the deeply satisfying religious feeling associated with the sweat lodge, the love of a remembered grandparent, the special taste of dry meat. Neither could the isolation, nor the periodic violence, nor the sense of loss and lack of control be shown in the restrictive format of a photograph.

Consequently it is impossible to tell, in photographic terms, the full story of the Blackfeet and the changes they have experienced as Indian people. These photographs, however, do evoke a feeling of closeness and understanding. It is no longer necessary to play fruitless, imaginative games as to what reservation life was like — now much of it, at least the exterior part, can be seen. And what is visible is Blackfeet people trying to cope with their changing world as Blackfeet. In the end, that is enough to justify this effort. As one young student, after spending an hour engrossed in that historical world, said knowingly as he looked up: "So that's what it was like."

*Spotted Eagle's camp with sun screen, 1890s*

Photo by Thomas Magee; courtesy of Angelo Greco

# Acknowledgments

LOCATING DISJOINTED SCRAPS, selecting bits and pieces of tribal life, arranging these into some semblance of order to give sense to the experience of American Indians is already an old, if not hoary, tradition. This effort at documenting the reservation Blackfeet continues the "rescue efforts" that occurred throughout the late nineteenth and early twentieth centuries as whole armies of painters, photographers, and ethnographers set out to preserve "before it was too late" tribal cultures. *The Reservation Blackfeet* participates in this elegiac movement and, as a salvage operation, my job has depended upon the work, the interest, and the active involvement of a great multitude. Thanking them in print and with the publication of this book is a pleasure I have looked forward to.

Thanks first to Gary Schmautz, my friend and collaborator, who collected photographs from all over the reservation, who sat with me when no one else would at the Heart Butte Round Hall, and whose help, sense of history, and support — public and private — could always be counted upon. From the beginning we worked together.

I am also grateful to Earl Barlow, former Superintendent of Browning School District No. 9. At the beginning when there were lots of "doubting Thomases," Earl Barlow believed. He pushed for funding and read the manuscript at various stages, making suggestive observations. His successor, Dr. Orville Dodge, continued that administrative support as did Tom Thompson and Superintendent Pat Conroy, both facilitating eventual publication. I appreciate their help.

Another debt of gratitude that I wish to acknowledge specifically is the one I owe to the two principal photographic donors: the Sherburne family (Fred, Doris, and Terry) of East Glacier; and William and Faith (Sherburne) Bercovich and Don and Peewee Magee of Browning.

The Thomas Magee photographs, with few exceptions, stem from the Magees' magnificent collection of negatives and prints. Don Magee, a former tribal councilman and curator with the Plains Indian Museum in Browning, believed in this photographic effort and placed his important collection at my disposal. Other researchers he had denied, but he helped me and I am grateful. Additionally, he rounded up photographs, put me into contact with knowledgeable people, and shed his own considerable historical light on knotty problems.

The Sherburne family graciously gave their extensive collection to the University of

## Blackfeet burial

Sometimes the Blackfeet buried their dead upon scaffolds built in cottonwood trees.
At other times the dead with their possessions were placed high upon the summit of a
butte or hill overlooking a broad sweep of the country. *Photo by Thomas Magee; courtesy of
Don Magee*

Montana Archives. Reflecting the family's more than half a century of intensive activity in trading, cattle, and banking, the J. H. and J. L. Sherburne Collection constitutes a significant historical resource. The Sherburnes were photographers of family and reservation as well, and their efforts, as can be seen in the photographic credits, were substantial.

For the expert help of Joe Bear Medicine I am grateful. He recognized early the need for a photographic "winter count," and he committed himself to helping whenever possible. Meeting with me at his house, often on the spur of the moment when I suddenly showed up in Browning, Joe Bear Medicine gave me his attention, his time, and his experience. He identified, instructed, and discussed. This book has profited immensely from his stimulating help. In so many ways, Joe Bear Medicine is my link to a Blackfeet past.

To those who contributed photographs that were not used in the book, my thanks.

Others to thank — the various members of the Johnson-O'Malley Committee as well as the Blackfeet Cultural Advisory Committee (Alex Sherman, Louise Evans, Kate Home Gun, Mary Little Bull, and Jenny Running Crane). Robert "Smokey" Rides-at-the-Door, Chairman of the JOM Committee that originally funded the project, pushed again and again for support. Later Dave Stevens, Jim Glaze, and Charlie Connelly helped. Charlie Connelly carefully read the manuscript, offering his views. Mary Ground (Grass Woman), Jim Reevis, Tom Many Guns, Louie Red Head, Joe Upham, and Peter Red Horn identified persons and places. Ursula Kramer coordinated the women at Mainstream. Mae Vallance, who spent wondrous years at Heart Butte during the thirties, loaned me her photographs, gave captions, and extended herself in other ways when it would have been easier not to. To Mae Crawford, my student and friend, I am also indebted.

Thanks too are in order for Hugh Dempsey of the Glenbow-Alberta Institute who generously read the manuscript and to Tom Newman and David Walter who likewise worked on earlier drafts. Peter Nabakov also helped me with the text. Jerry Kling, John Well-Off-Man, and Director Devon Chandler of Instructional Materials Service at the University of Montana did all of the photographic reproductions with care, precision, and craft. Again and again they redid work until it was exactly right — pulling out detail, improving, giving the photographs a quality others thought impossible. Thanks too go to Kathy Schaefer and Dale Johnson of the University of Montana Archives and Special Collections for their help with difficult bibliographic searches.

I have also enjoyed the benefit of the very professional staff at the University of Washington Press. Editors Naomi Pascal and Julidta Tarver guided this protracted project with kind words and demanding scholarly standards. Their belief in this book and its value, and their patience with my meandering pace, was the tonic I often needed. They did not lose faith. Lane Morgan and Audrey Meyer with their imaginative eyes saw and gave an extra dimension, and I appreciate their contribution.

And then there is Julie — Julie McVay, our departmental secretary, who is so much more than what that title indicates. She has typed, typed, and typed again my often confusing prose, my illegible handwriting, my interminable insertions and additions with patience, a critical eye, and above all with humor and helpfulness. And while she may not have kissed this frog of a manuscript into a prince, she has transformed it and I thank her.

To the unnamed others who have helped in ways great and small, who gave a boost, my gratitude is equally there — even if unregistered.

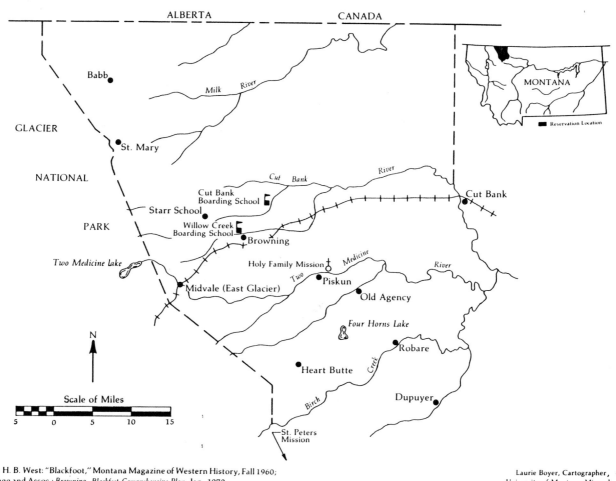

# THE BLACKFEET RESERVATION

ALBERTA  CANADA

MONTANA

Reservation Location

Babb

*Milk River*

GLACIER

St. Mary

NATIONAL

*Cut Bank*  River  Cut Bank

Cut Bank
Boarding School

Starr School

Willow Creek
Boarding School

PARK  Browning

*Two Medicine lake*

Holy Family Mission  *Medicine River*

*Two*

Midvale (East Glacier)  Piskun

Old Agency

N  *Four Horns Lake*

Robare

*Creek*

Heart Butte

Dupuyer

Scale of Miles

5   0   5   10   15

*Birch*

St. Peters
Mission

Source: H. B. West: "Blackfoot," Montana Magazine of Western History, Fall 1960;
H. G. Fagg and Assoc.: *Browning- Blackfeet Comprehensive Plan*, Jan. 1970.

Laurie Boyer, Cartographer,  4/84
University of Montana, Missoula, MT

# BLACKFEET RESERVATION BOUNDARY
# CHANGES, 1873 TO PRESENT

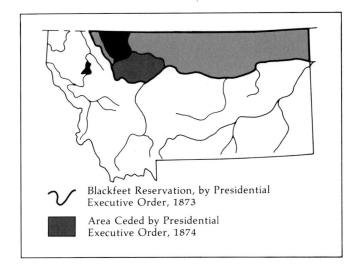

~ Blackfeet Reservation, by Presidential
Executive Order, 1873

▮ Area Ceded by Presidential
Executive Order, 1874

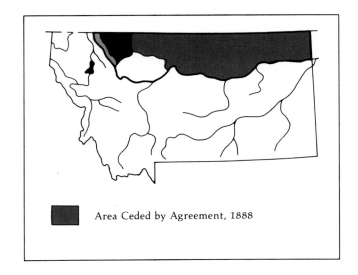

▮ Area Ceded by Agreement, 1888

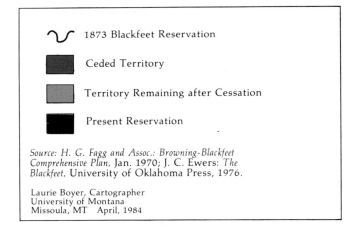

~ 1873 Blackfeet Reservation

▮ Ceded Territory

▮ Territory Remaining after Cessation

▮ Present Reservation

*Source: H. G. Fagg and Assoc.: Browning-Blackfeet
Comprehensive Plan, Jan. 1970; J. C. Ewers: The
Blackfeet, University of Oklahoma Press, 1976.*

Laurie Boyer, Cartographer
University of Montana
Missoula, MT   April, 1984

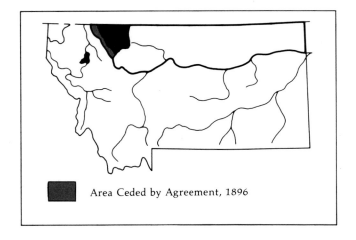

▮ Area Ceded by Agreement, 1896

# The End of the Buffalo Days

IT IS EASY to believe, as you drive across the billowing grasslands that run north in a great sweep along the edge of the Continental Divide, that little has changed since the turn of the century. The Rocky Mountains still wall up the sky, the wind still blows free, uninhibited by shelter belts or tractor sheds, and the high prairie still seems to change only with the color of the seasons. Time appears to have rested here before tracking on.

The traditional landmarks remain in place, points along the jagged horizon. To the north stands Chief Mountain, a broken prow that is at once the easternmost extension of the Rocky Mountains and the signpost of the Canadian border. In the center of the panorama rises Divide Mountain, a rock shed, spilling water north to Hudson's Bay and south to the Missouri River and Gulf of Mexico. Bordering Divide Mountain to the south is Cut Bank Ridge, a gravel line pushing out onto the plains. Finally, curled around on the far southern rim of the expanse, is low-slung Heart Butte. These promontories continue to impart to the traveler a sense of place in this undulating ocean of grass that is the Blackfeet Indian Reservation of northcentral Montana.

This open, free land is broken only by a few scattered communities, by a passing pickup with Glacier County's "38" license plates, or by an occasional solitary fence line, which only emphasizes the general lack of fencing. It is land distinct from the heavily cultivated and structured wheat fields just east of the reservation, and the tidy farms, with their patterned, geometric fields, across the Canadian line. This is exotic country. It can overwhelm the senses and trigger the historical imagination.

Traveling from the southeast — from Valier, or Conrad, or Dupuyer — the reservation boundary is conspicuous: the road hunches its shoulders and narrows, telephone lines dwindle away, and grasslands, clear and free, begin to dominate. At night the twinkling brilliance of numerous farmhouse windows and yard lights suddenly slips away in the rearview mirror, leaving only a few glimmers isolated here and there. It becomes appreciably darker. This Indian land is more natural, less restrained, than the pampered farmland to the southeast, to the east, and to the north.

From the west via U.S. #2, after running the tourist traps, the bars, and the garish signs of the communities bordering Glacier National Park — Hungry Horse, Martin City, Coram — the traveler weaves through the west side, passing West Glacier Park, moving up the canyon of the Middle Fork of the Flathead, down to Walton, around the corner, and up Bear Creek to Marias Pass. By then everything has changed: skyline, vegetation, wind, and rock color all point to the plains and the east side of the mountains. Crossing the reservation line just east of the pass near the old Lubec Ranger Station, the traveler bursts out upon the edge of the plains, into grass, and a horizon that runs beyond sight.

Reservation land is a continuous, unceasing monotone of exposed plains, contours, abrasions, and streams. The dun color laps over the grazing land, through the aspen fields of the foothills, and up into the windy rock at the top of the continent. Wind and weather push the reservation people around, guiding if not controlling their actions.

This is a country conducive to historical dreams. Here the memory of man runs a shorter course than in most places. If you squint, instead of seeing scattered cattle adrift in the grass-filled, potholed land, you dimly can see trailing buffalo and buffalo people. They are very close here — so close that it is almost a question of listening. Yet this feeling of historical proximity can be terribly deceptive, however alluring and mysterious. For things *have* changed here.

Prior to the mid-nineteenth century, the Blackfeet dominated that portion of the upper Great Plains north of the Missouri River and east of the Rocky Mountains. Blackfeet existence depended upon hunting the migrating buffalo and, particularly after the development of the horse culture in the early eighteenth century, on raiding neighboring tribes. The buffalo focused this meandering life, connecting activities and providing their meaning, while always supplying the principal source of food and material wealth.

The Blackfeet people comprised four major, closely related tribes: the Siksika or Blackfoot proper; the Kainah or Blood; the Northern Pikuni or Northern Piegan; the Southern Pikuni or Southern Piegan. Rivals at times but never enemies, each tribe endeavored to protect and promote its special sense of identity. Together these Blackfeet maintained a common language, unifying customs, and similar religious beliefs. Often their members intermarried; frequently they united to hunt, to fight, or to celebrate as related peoples joined in a common enterprise. This constant intermingling, the shared rhythm of nomadic life spent in small bands, and the communal reliance upon the buffalo, forged lasting bonds. From this common experience developed a reality, a traditional collective consciousness specific to the Blackfeet.

Even prior to the celebrated 1806 encounter between Meriwether Lewis and a small group of Piegans, the Blackfeet had been influenced by an advancing white civilization. Because European fashion required a steady supply of beaver pelts for gentlemen's hats, the Hudson's Bay Company had expanded a fur-trading empire across North America, replete with trading posts, exchange goods, and new economic and transport systems. The British enterprises soon were challenged in the Upper Missouri region by competing American companies, which used the Missouri to reduce transport costs. Still, the Blackfeet's isolation and hostile reputation minimized their involvement in the beaver trade.

Only after 1830, with the fashion decline of the beaver hat, did the Blackfeet become engaged seriously in white commerce. As American manufacturers discovered additional uses for the buffalo hide, the Blackfeet became an integral link in the robe trade. They not only controlled a vast portion of the northern Great Plains, on which the herds grazed, but they also found the commercial hunting of buffalo compatible with their own hunting tradition. American fur companies based in St. Louis located fur forts throughout the Upper Missouri region, relying upon the Missouri River for the downriver transport of the heavy robes. Fort Union, near the confluence of the Yellowstone and the Missouri rivers, and Fort Benton, above the mouth of the Marias, soon proved the kingpins of a river transport system for this hide commerce.

The buffalo robe trade involved a new dependence of the American trader upon the Indian hunter. The Blackfeet — applying the horse and the gun, and spurred by economic reward — adjusted readily to the requirements of an enterprise that featured the hunter rather than the trapper. The buffalo trade permitted the Blackfeet to maintain their traditional enthusiasm for the hunt and to continue their established social and religious customs. Only the material rewards had multiplied. The new enterprise, however, did produce some changes in the existing patterns. Because of the increased volume of hides that required treatment, Blackfeet women became more involved in the production process. An adjustment also was necessary in the traditional hunting concept that emphasized harvesting only what buffalo could be used by a band's members.

The accelerated hide trade encouraged the Blackfeet hunting bands to increase both their size and efficiency and to expand their territory. As a result, the tribes acquired a surplus of traditional buffalo hunt items, such as meat, horses, clothing, utensils, and weapons. To this accumulated wealth was added the white man's trade items: blankets, wagons, cotton and wool clothing, beads, brass tacks, buttons, badges, handkerchiefs, thimbles, and, most important, guns. Yet, just as the buffalo trade augmented the Blackfeet's material wealth, so it inexorably drew them into the white economic system, which proved the harbinger of ever-growing white pressure on the Blackfeet culture.

In 1855 the United States government, in response to eastern desires to push west, concluded its first treaty dealing directly with the Blackfeet tribes of Montana and Canada. Known as Lame Bull's Treaty, it was negotiated with "The Blackfoot Nation," a collective body made up of Piegans, Bloods, and Northern Blackfeet, as well as their close neighbors and allies, the Gros Ventres. Commissioners Alfred Cumming and Isaac I. Stevens sought to gradually end the incessant intertribal warfare on the Upper Missouri, and the best way seemed to be a treaty with the Blackfeet tribes that would limit their sphere of influence to an area north of a line drawn from the continental divide directly east to the Musselshell River and then wiggling down river to where the Milk River mouths into the Missouri. Once peace prevailed between the tribes and the Blackfeet warriors remained in their territory, construction of a great transcontinental rail line across the Northern Great Plains could begin, bringing the inevitable white flood of settlement.

The Blackfeet chiefs, led by Lame Bull, agreed to the treaty on October 16, 1855. The terms gave the Blackfeet $20,000 "in useful goods and services" annually for ten years as well as an additional $15,000 each year to promote their "civilization and Christianization" through instructional farms, schools, and agricultural equipment. For their part the Blackfeet promised perpetual peace with the United States and an end to intertribal warfare; they also limited themselves to an exclusive territory north of the Hellgate-Musselshell River-Milk River line to the south and east, and they agreed to allow U.S. citizens to live in and travel through their lands. Finally, the Blackfeet were to permit the construction of all types of roads, telegraph lines, military posts, missions, schools, and, of course, government agencies.

In order to distribute the annual goods and services promised in Lame Bull's Treaty, the United States established an agency under the direction of Edwin A. C. Hatch at Fort Benton. Huddled under the protective bluffs of the Upper Missouri River, this river port was the focus of white activity in the entire region, as well as the center of the collective tribal territory. It was the logical place to distribute the treaty annuities.

The Bloods, the Northern Blackfeet, and a small number of Piegan generally lived north of the boundary between the United States and Canada, yet they crossed the forty-ninth parallel at will to hunt, socialize, and, of course, to receive the annuities from the United States government. The Southern Piegan, later designated the Blackfeet of Montana, accepted their northern confederates from across the "medicine line" as themselves. Lame Bull's Treaty lumped them all together; later history, however, sorted them out so that by the late 1880s only the Southern Piegan, the Montana Blackfeet, lived in the United States.

Hatch reported in his abbreviated way that in 1856 he distributed treaty annuities to about eight thousand Indians. The gathered Blackfeet seemed to think of the annuities as free gifts and their distribution initiated a great surge south. In most cases these goods essentially duplicated items already available through the buffalo robe trade or they stretched the treaty definition of "useful goods" to include coffee and rice, which Blackfeet disliked, and moldy pilot bread shipped west from St. Louis. The annuities, however, did promote an effort to educate, as the treaty promised, and it did so through a developing pattern of agency intervention and dependency that would have grave consequences after the buffalo were gone.

After 1855 Fort Benton bubbled with commercial activity as it focused white activity in the Blackfeet lands. Not surprisingly, this merchant mecca ignored the Blackfeet bands themselves as much as it could. From 1859–60 was Fort Benton not only the head of navigation for shallow-draft steamers puffing up the Missouri, but it connected the Missouri lifeline to the Columbia River and the Pacific Northwest via the Mullan road. After 1862, wagon roads feeding the gold camps to the south and west only provided additional spokes to Fort Benton's warehousing, distributing, and freighting hub.

Whiskey traders, wolfers, prospectors, merchant princes, freighters, and settlers constituted a sprawling white population that feared the Blackfeet bands. Growing hostility and numerous small incidents fed white fears. By 1867 settlers along the Sun River demanded and received protection with the rapid erection of Fort Shaw, manned by a troop of "blue coats."

As Fort Benton thrived in the late 1860s, its leading merchants diversified their operations, specifically by investing in livestock operations. Joining established Montana stockmen and enterprising white immigrants, they threw large herds onto the high, grassy plains that fed a decreasing number of buffalo. The Blackfeet lands, negotiated in 1855 at Lame Bull's Treaty, attracted increasing white attention as stockmen required more open-range grazing. The result was two Executive Orders, signed by President Ulysses S. Grant in 1873 and 1874, which moved the reservation's southern boundary north of the Missouri and Marias rivers and Birch Creek. This reduction in land neither required nor received Blackfeet endorsement, and the federal government offered no payment. The diminution of the reservation, however, did accelerate a form of guerrilla warfare that some Blackfeet bands had waged since the 1860s against the flood of white intruders.

Skirmishes, isolated killings, property losses, and harassment affected both whites and Indians. Violent actions, often severe but only sporadic, involved few individuals, yet any aggressive Blackfeet act provoked loud demands from the white majority for military protection. The combination of white insecurity and the white coveting of Blackfeet lands resulted in 1870 in a mistaken cavalry attack on a friendly Blackfeet camp. The Baker Massacre — on Heavy Runner's smallpox-devastated band, huddled on the Marias River in subzero weather — left 173 Blackfeet dead and 140 women and children driven into the Montana elements. The Blackfeet tribes, bewildered by the army's action and divided by indecision, mounted no reprisal. In the 1870s, peace finally descended on the Blackfeet for a reason that White Calf best expressed: "Further war would only result in our extermination." Already the total Blackfeet population had dropped below three thousand, and waves of settlers disembarking annually at the Fort Benton levee continued to inflate the white majority.

The Blackfeet north of the "medicine line" fared better at the hands of their government. The arrival of the North West Mounted Police in 1874 rapidly concluded the whiskey trade that had operated out of Fort Benton through numerous fur forts on the Crown's land. Then in 1877 the Canadian government negotiated Treaty Number Seven with the Northern Blackfeet, the Bloods, and the Northern Piegan. The tribes relinquished title to their hunting grounds and agreed to specific reserves, for "both their benefit and confinement"; the government promised annuities, cattle, agricultural tools, ammunition, and schools.

By the end of the 1870s, a relative equilibrium had evolved on each side of the forty-ninth parallel. On both sides, Indian people had lost their legal rights to vast amounts of territory; on both sides, treaties had created new situations rather than recognizing old ones. Peace was established. Territory was defined and reserved for the nominal confinement of the several Blackfeet tribes. Rights, delegations, annuities, and above all, limitations, were defined in legal terms. Jurisdiction, sovereignty, and citizenship became important considerations for the Blackfeet. With the application of white legal definitions of the Blackfeet and their lands, the American-Canadian border became a line of real significance, dividing what had been a single people.

The American Blackfeet needed a fairly even Indian-white population ratio and the existence of the buffalo to continue their traditional life. Neither was a permanent feature. The 1880 federal census listed approximately 2,200 Blackfeet, and a white population in Choteau, Lewis and Clark, and Meagher counties alone of more than 12,000 persons.

In addition, a vastly expanded open-range cattle industry impinged on Blackfeet lands and on the dwindling buffalo herds.

Cattle were competing for range with buffalo, and were winning, but the Blackfeet hunted successfully through 1880 and 1881. Because of this success, Indian agent John W. Young, located at Old Agency on lower Badger Creek, reported that he could not convince the bands "to give up their nomadic life and settle down to farm or raise cattle."

With the last herds of buffalo, the Blackfeet wandered their shrinking world, despite the white voices telling them to abandon the hunt. Then, just as the tribes were beginning to adjust to their diminished reservation lands, the great stretches of horizon, rippled by ridges and shallow coulees, became barren. Abruptly the buffalo were gone. The Blackfeet, the buffalo people, continued to look in the dun expanse of changing light but they spotted little other than competing tribesmen from the north and east. Breaking into smaller and smaller bands to cover more country, the American Blackfeet both rushed and straggled from one favorite haunt to another. Wherever they went their camp followers were there — whiskey traders, white horse thieves, hide merchants. Usually they were pushed, too, as they traveled, squeezed here or there by a settler's wire fence, a rancher's Winchester, or patrolling military squads. There were no buffalo kills. With their situation deteriorating, often threatened, becoming ragged and hungry, the Piegan buffalo hunters one by one decided to turn around and to start the long, sad way back west to the government rations of Old Agency waiting under the shroud of the Rockies.

Strung out at varying intervals along the winding bottoms of Badger, Little Badger, and Birch creeks, the Blackfeet hunting bands turned sedentary in the extreme southern portion of their still large reservation. With no game to chase, no robe trade to absorb the impact, the Blackfeet hungered and waited for the Indian agent at Old Agency to distribute the goods and rations owed them by treaty arrangement. Even this last resort failed. The rations were not delivered and the bewildered Blackfeet, often plagued by small pox too, starved gruesomely. In the Starvation Winter of 1883–84 an estimated six hundred died.

With the eradication of the buffalo, the gradual social adaptation of the Blackfeet that had been based upon Indian-white exchange and cultural choice was no longer possible. Whatever parity might have existed between the two cultures evaporated with the disappearance of the economic base, the buffalo. It was also soured by white encroachment, then by disease, by alcohol, and, of course, by confinement away from their Canadian relatives. Isolated, losing numerical force, and pushed into dependency by hunger, Blackfeet people had lost their chance at gradual accommodation. What would develop in its place was the raw, abrupt substitution of a white world for an Indian one. The buffalo culture no longer existed, no longer provided a viable alternative. Change had arrived, wrecking the Blackfeet world. As they became reservation Indians their loss only grew and yet it was so difficult to assess by European immigrant standards. It was more than a loss of a way of life, but was, confusing as it may sound, a loss of home in their own homeland. Now nothing could be taken for granted. There were at once too many choices and yet no choice. The Blackfeet had begun their reservation stay.

# After the Buffalo:

## *Old Agency on Badger Creek*

THE PHOTOGRAPHIC HISTORY of the Blackfeet began in the years immediately following the starvation tragedy. Reduced to some two thousand, the Blackfeet survived — but barely. A number of warrior fathers and their families tried gardening, challenging not only their inexperience and disdain but also the early and late frosts that settled in the cottonwood bottoms. If frosts did not stunt the feeble crops, they were shriveled by blasts of a hot summer wind that never entirely stopped. The strange effort of digging with a steel shovel and the ridicule of relatives further diminished the garden's promise. It was easier to hunt for imaginary game in something like the old way, and to count on the ration ticket that had to be punched when Saturday rolled around and the family travois or wagon traced the other tracks leading to the agency.

Away to the north and the east the reservation was an almost empty expanse of light and growing grass, now that the buffalo were gone. The reservation herds were few; aside from the agency herd that supplied weekly beef, there were only scattered bunches belonging to individual Blackfeet or to white men who had married Piegan wives. White cattlemen looked with envy and greed on these grasslands in motion. Not content to simply look or to trespass by grazing what came to be thousands of sheep, horses, and cattle on Indian land, these same exploiters marshaled other white commercial interests, initiating a succession of ingenious political plans to open up the reservation to further white settlement and use. A great deal of confusion compounded the boundary questions, but no one paid much attention. Given the level of illegal white use, that seemed hardly necessary.

Following the starvation period the political pressure on the reservation boundaries intensified. Letters streamed in to Congressmen, Montana delegates cornered influential politicians, and hometown newspapers featured editorial blasts. The *Helena Herald* stormed that "these ranges are needed for our cattle and they are of no use in the world to the Indians." When Congress did not respond quickly enough to further reservation reductions, stockmen tried yet another tack — continuing to graze their herds on Indian land through a permit system.

By 1885, with good reason, white Montanans anticipated a final and complete access to reservation land. James Hill's Great Northern Railroad had mobilized a large amount of support for such action; realization depended in fact upon the railroad's ability to open the northern Great Plains to unprecedented development. An economic juggernaut loomed on the edge of the future, exciting stockmen, miners, settlers, and merchants. The Blackfeet were too few and too vulnerable to stand in the way.

Late in 1886 Congress appointed a new Treaty Commission to negotiate with the Blackfeet, the Sioux, the Assiniboine, and the Gros Ventres. Subject — land sale. Meeting with the Treaty Commission in early February 1887, in extreme cold and for only five short days, the Blackfeet elders led by White Calf and Three Sons, so pliable in their immediate concerns, signed a treaty that gave away most of their land. The entire eastern portion of the earlier reservation was abandoned and the Blackfeet restricted and contained in a small, rectangular space, hard under the Rockies. The new border began at Cut Bank Creek where it entered the Marias River, ran north to the 49th parallel, then turned west and followed, surveyor-straight, the "medicine line" to the mountain tops of the Continental Divide. It zigzagged south along that edge to Birch Creek, and then, with an almost ninety degree turn, flowed with Birch Creek back to the starting point on the Marias.

In return for this loss of land which many remembered as the time "when we sold the Sweet Grass Hills," the Blackfeet received collectively $150,000 annually for ten years to purchase livestock and equipment, to build schools and homes that would lead the tribe, now numbering less than two thousand, to economic independence and cultural assimilation.

Realization of these twin goals depended principally upon the desires of Indian families, yet the Blackfeet had had little voice in establishing them. Whatever the annual payment, however suitable for grazing the well-watered reservation lands might be, the failure to involve the Blackfeet in determining their own economic goals proved to be a recurring handicap.

Another obstacle was the local Indian agent assigned to implement government policy while protecting the Blackfeet and their complicated interests. With understanding and compassion, the local agent was to nudge the Blackfeet closer and closer toward "useful, civilized, Christian lives." To accomplish this the agent assessed the separate and local needs of families: he reviewed prevailing conditions, measured levels of ability and activity, and then he proceeded to plan comprehensively for both the present and the future. It was complicated prophecy. It also had to be done within the context of a limited budget — namely the annual payment the Blackfeet received from the U.S. government for tribal land. One knowledgeable historian has written that such an agent had to resemble "Moses, who would lead his children out of the bondage of ignorance and poverty." Unfortunately no Moses existed for the Blackfeet. What they got instead were seven different agents in the fourteen-year period between 1886 and 1900.

These agents, always poorly paid, acquired their positions through a system of political patronage that drew upon a reservoir of losers and guaranteed a high turnover. For most, the main concern during a brief tenure was to capitalize on the opportunities presented by their dominant position on the reservation. And to a man, the Blackfeet agents had either too much or too little experience with the Piegan and northern Montana. One extreme was as bad as the other. Year after year, Blackfeet agents and their growing administrative staffs simply stole, swindled, or wasted away the annual tribal income aimed at providing for the Piegan future. Government tutelage degenerated into a form of organized fraud, and the Blackfeet knew it. They had traded away magnificent land for minimal food and support; now they watched their trust being squandered away.

With too many agents and too many policies, for policy changed as rapidly as agents, Blackfeet opportunities were lost through conflict and confusion. One agent overturned the work of another and a third duplicated the efforts of the first. By the late summer months of 1895, the Blackfeet, through no fault of their own, were again forced to trade their only commodity — land — for additional support. Economic self-sufficiency remained a dream for the future. Nearly ten years and over $1.5 million dollars had been expended by the government agents on irrigation ditches, sawmills, schools, a tribal cattle herd, and an enlarged agency staff. The Blackfeet, however, had little to show for it.

The economic success that eluded the Blackfeet in the early 1890s was bestowed, however, on many of the whites who continued to exploit even the reduced Indian land. Numerous prospectors blasted and dug illegally for gold, silver, and copper in the western section of the reservation, along the foothills and in the high, alpine valleys just under the Continental Divide. There was also continued cattle trespass as white ranchers drove their herds onto reservation grasslands or simply shipped them to isolated railroad sidings just outside the reservation line and then allowed them to "drift" over. Agents could not or would not stop this illegal activity.

Coinciding with the growing Indian need for money was the ever-present public demand to abolish the whole reservation. Underscoring and supporting this sentiment, the Great Northern Railroad streaked across the reservation in the early 1890s; eastern interest and investment in Montana multiplied in leaps. Yet the coming of the railroad also stimulated the development of an Indian cattle industry. Individual Blackfeet families tried their hand at raising large numbers of cattle for eastern markets and many of their tentative ventures showed a profit. Prior to 1900 Blackfeet ranchers registered over five hundred brands and operated over "two hundred mowing machines to cut wild hay for winter cattle feed." The Blackfeet cattle industry looked promising.

The presence of the Great Northern not only encouraged stockmen, but also helped to shift the geographic focus of the tribe. After the treaty of 1887, Old Agency on Badger Creek became less central to tribal life. Many families had chosen to strike out on their own away from the traditional bands, settling further to the north in the protective river bottoms of Two Medicine River, Cut Bank Creek, and Willow Creek. Underneath the steep, grassy bluffs that dropped from the flat plains and isolated ridges, these bottomlands offered water, protection from the incessant wind, and a chance to build a cottonwood cabin and to put in a little garden.

The Blackfeet spread out. To accommodate the population shift to the north a new clapboard and brick boarding school was built in 1892 above the gravel of Willow Creek some twenty miles north of Old Agency. Agent Captain Lorenzo W. Cooke found the arrival of the railroad to the north an immense benefit in administering the reservation, and he wanted to be closer. He proposed moving the site of the agency north to Willow Creek, the railroad and the boarding school. In 1893 permission arrived from Washington, D.C., and by 1895 the new agency — twenty buildings constructed with Indian money and considerable Blackfeet labor — was complete. Only one step was left for the reservation to be ready for the twentieth century — a final land sale.

While the Blackfeet and their agent tried to secure some advantage from the arrival of the Great Northern, mining interests continued to press the government to open the east side of the Rocky Mountains up to mineral claim. Cooke's successor, Agent George Steell, supported these efforts as did George Bird Grinnell, editor of *Field and Stream* and a knowledgeable and interested friend of the Blackfeet since 1888. In the late winter of 1895 a Blackfeet delegation of thirty-one elders agreed to negotiate the sale of the mountainous western portion of their reservation. By September, George Bird Grinnell and two other appointed treaty commissioners, William C. Pollock and Walter M. Clements, finally reached a compromise price for the strip of "ceded land" that was to become part of Glacier National Park. The United States government was to pay another $1.5 million over another ten-year period. The Blackfeet by selling more land opted for a second chance at independence, a second chance to develop that elusive economic base so desperately needed for survival in the twentieth century.

Hope, accompanying government drafts, again threaded its way among those Blackfeet, the majority, who had not been able to participate initially in the cattle prosperity. Ten years had passed since the last sale of land; more people had settled down, had gained greater experience as stockmen, and a few had even learned to farm. Now by utilizing the money generated by the sale of the "mineral strip" to develop a grazing economy, they had a chance to make it. Although their reservation had shrunk beyond the recognition of the elders, the Blackfeet were ready for the twentieth century.

*Issuing old clothing at Old Agency, 1880s*

In 1876 the "Four Persons" Agency near Choteau on the Teton River had to be abandoned because the reservation boundary had been moved arbitrarily by Executive Order in 1873 and 1874, leaving the Blackfeet Agency far south and off the reduced Blackfeet lands. The agency was moved to Badger Creek under the supervision of Agent John Young with the aid of the Blackfeet themselves. Women and men dug cellars and hauled stones and finally lime from deposits near Heart Butte. This new agency came to be called "Old Agency," or in Piegan "Old Ration Place," when the government began issuing supplies to the starving, destitute Blackfeet following the disappearance of the buffalo in 1883. *Photo courtesy of Tim Gordon*

## Issue day for beef rations at Blackfeet Agency

With the plains country almost barren, the Blackfeet congregated around "Old Ration Place," where tribal money acquired through land sales bought white-man's rations. Each man, woman, and child was to receive one-and-one-half pounds of meat, half a pound of flour, and small amounts of beans, bacon, salt, soda, and coffee each week. Reality, however, was more grim and hunger a constant threat. Families wasted nothing of the rations — offal, tripe, head meat, hooves, and marrow bones were piled and divided. The burial ground above to the east, "Ghost Ridge," reminded the surviving that some six hundred Piegan had frozen or starved a year or two before. *Photo courtesy of Montana Historical Society*

*Reaching for entrails at the agency slaughterhouse, 1887*

Blackfeet cattle were at first slaughtered out in the open, but agency officials later decided this procedure was too similar to buffalo hunting to be sanitary and civilized. A government slaughterhouse was built, and cattle from the agency herd were butchered on Friday and issued on Saturday. *Courtesy of UM Archives*

## Old Agency on Badger Creek, 1898

By the late 1880s the Blackfeet identified more with their agency than ever before. Not only had their treaty monies paid for it, they had helped with the actual building, and it had, after considerable bungling, saved them from starvation. Ironically, the agency's design, with a stockade, compound, and two watch towers at diagonal corners, was that of a hostile fort, and the staff did little to alter that impression. Amid the collapsed world of the Blackfeet past, the agency was a strange and inescapable white island that contained farm instructors, schools, teachers, doctors, interpreters, stores, and living quarters for agency employees. *Photo by J. H. Sherburne; courtesy of Sherburne Collection, UM Archives*

## Agency employees at Old Agency, 1891

Where did these hard, tough men come from? Many had had experience in the fur and whiskey trade and had remained in Blackfeet country piecing together a living. Others were ex-army men, drifters, men down on their luck, or "squaw men" willing to put up with the dictatorial supervision of the agent for a small salary and a chance to exploit. Hired to help the Blackfeet move into a new and changing world, this agency circle tried halfheartedly to teach the Blackfeet to farm, to use machinery, to manage with English and numbers. Educating was an enormous task even for capable, dedicated men; given the deplorable conditions at Old Agency, the quality of local white help, and inept administrative appointments, it was an impossible task. Army Lieutenant John Beacom, investigating complaints in 1891, took this photograph to document the number of employees, not the quality of their work. *Photo by Lt. John Beacom; courtesy of Southwest Museum*

*Piegan braves at Big Badger Creek Agency, ca. 1886 or 1887*

Left to right: Tom Horn, Good Gun, Yellow Kidney, Medicine Bull, unidentified, Swims Under, unidentified, unidentified.

The Piegan numbered some two thousand in 1889, and to a degree the starvation winter of 1883 had been overcome — they now had food, blankets, and clothing and were negotiating for greater amounts of supplies. *Photo by A. B. Coe; courtesy of Smithsonian Institution*

*White Calf, chief of the Piegans, at Old Agency, ca. 1886*

The traditional chiefs, including head chief White Calf, tried to cope with the forced change of life. Retaining a measure of authority independent of the growing power of the white agent, these leaders struggled to find ways to meet the needs of their people. White Calf, who had the reputation of being overly cooperative with the white agency, believed the Blackfeet had no other choice. *Photo probably by A. B. Coe; courtesy of MSU Archives*

INDIAN PALACE CAR

*Indian palace car outside Old Agency, 1899*

On Saturdays families saddled up their horses or hitched up their wagons to make the weekly trek to Old Agency. "The stockade itself and all the government buildings are whitewashed and glisten with a dazzling effect in the strong sunlight at noonday. Just inside the outer gate is a cozy little lookout from which the guard obtains a clear and unobstructed view of the Indian village of Piegan, distant perhaps half a mile." *Photo by Thomas Magee; courtesy of Angelo Grego*

## Agency school at Badger Creek, 1890

The Catholic Jesuits, or Black Robes, established St. Peter's Mission in 1859 near present day Choteau on the Teton River and were the first whites to attempt the education of the Blackfeet. The first government school opened its doors at the Teton River agency in 1872 but had little success in attracting pupils who were too busy hunting and traveling. After the 1870 Baker Massacre in which Heavy Runner's band of peaceful Piegan were annihilated by U.S. soldiers from Ft. Shaw, Congress decided upon a radical shift in general Indian policy; it would practice peace rather than war. Part of the "Peace Policy" was a more determined attempt to educate Blackfeet children. By 1890 the Old Agency day school had a superintendent, A. B. Coe, and one additional teacher. There were thirty-nine students, many of them children of white agency employees and mixed bloods. This government enterprise came to compete with missionary schools off the reservation and government boarding schools. *Photo by Lt. John Beacom; courtesy of Southwest Museum*

*Preceptress at Old Agency, 1887*

An elegant Victorian lady teacher attempted to establish contact with the local women. Black satin dress, a fringed parasol, and ribbons, however, reflected a definition of life so different as to be incomprehensible. *Photo courtesy of Nora Spanish*

*Blackfeet boys brought to St. Peter's by Father Imoda, 1885*

St. Peter's Mission had been left more than sixty miles south of the reservation when the boundary was moved north in 1874. As the school at the new agency could not meet the increasing demand, many Blackfeet families sent their children to St. Peter's.

Various denominations were involved in reviewing and recommending prospective agents for the reservations and were also given missionary responsibilities on specific reservations. The Methodist Church received the Blackfeet even though the Jesuits had worked successfully among them for more than a quarter of a century. The result was a serious rift between Agent John Young, a Methodist minister, and the Catholic fathers Peter Prando and John Imoda. Both factions actively recruited Blackfeet children. Because St. Peter's was off the reservation, Young termed Catholic recruitment as "abduction" and claimed that only he was the tutor and guardian of Indian children — not their parents, who often consented to Black Robe schooling. By the Starvation Winter, Young managed to have the Jesuits banned from the reservation. Prando, unwilling to give up his missionary work, built a small mission complex just across the reservation boundary on the south side of Birch Creek. *Courtesy of UM Archives*

## First Communion at Holy Family Mission, ca. 1898

In 1887 Chief White Calf, who had been baptized by Father Prando in 1882, responded to meet the needs of his own by contributing land on Two Medicine River. There, under the dun bluffs, Father Damiani and three Ursuline sisters built and opened a mission school, Holy Family, in 1890. With few exceptions the students spent the entire year at the school. They did not go home for holidays and parents were not allowed to visit, although Lizzie Henderson recalled that "the families of the children would camp in the bush and kids would visit them on holidays." The purpose of the students' isolation, of course, was for the school to break down the old habits, to convert them to "civilization," by eradicating traditional languages, values, and daily practices. *Photo by Thomas Magee; courtesy of Don Magee*

## Holy Family Mission Band

Horns, drums, and cymbals combined with uniforms, buttoned collars, and laced shoes to measure a new pride, allowing these pupils to demonstrate the freshness with which they approached their present.

The curriculum at Holy Family was vocational and spiritual as well as academic. Mary Ground remembered that "you started with the ABCs, learning to write and speak English at the same time. School was from grade one through grade five. . . . You had three good meals a day and a clean place to sleep. I worked in the kitchen and bakery." *Photo by Thomas Magee; courtesy of Oregon Provincial Archives, Society of Jesus, Gonzaga University*

*Old John Monroe, ca. 1905*          *Charley Chouquette*

White presence and influence on the Blackfeet Reservation ballooned following the Civil War and the Gold Rush of the 1870s. One of the more colorful newcomers was Hugh Monroe, known as Rising Wolf, who mastered the Blackfeet language, married Sinopah, daughter of Lone Walker, and became an established trapper, guide, and rancher. John Monroe, his half-blood son, expanded his cattle interests into the empty grazing lands north of Two Medicine River. *Photo by Thomas Magee; courtesy of Smithsonian Institution*

Charley Chouquette (born 1818 near St. Louis), along with Baptiste Rodin, Louis Nequette, and Charles Rivois, worked for Pierre Choteau's American Fur Company. His experiences included a hair-raising escape from unfriendly Crow Indians. He married a Piegan woman, Rosa Lee, and lived by farming and stock-raising in the Sun River Valley before moving to the reservation prior to 1900. Agency employees, ex–fur traders, and cowboys often married local Piegan women and created a mixed-blood community of Monroes, Henkels, Uphams, Kennerlys, Kipps, and Crofts, to name but a few. These "squaw men" gained acceptance on the reservation. Often they aggressively expanded their cattle operations to take advantage of the reservation grass now available because of their wives' status as tribal members. *Photo by Thomas Magee; courtesy of Don Magee*

## Joe Kipp

Perhaps the most extraordinary white man among the Blackfeet was Joe Kipp, or Raven Quiver. He began his career as an employee of the American Fur Company, and later scouted for the U.S. Army, leading the troops from Fort Shaw under Major Eugene Baker that massacred Heavy Runner's band on the Marias River in 1870. After venturing into whiskey running and merchandising in Canada, Kipp became a licensed Indian trader in Robare and later in Browning. Robare was a little stopping spot on Birch Creek that lived off bartering illegal whiskey, guns, and ammunition to the Blackfeet.

Always resourceful, always colorful, always on the edge of the law, Kipp kept everyone's respect. The "merchant prince of the Upper Missouri" asserted that he had attended every treaty council held with the Piegan Indians except the first with Governor Stevens in 1855–56. His self-interest demanded it. *Photo courtesy of MSU Archives*

## Tom Dawson, ca. 1910

Like Joe Kipp, Charley Chouquette, and Charley Rivois, Dawson was linked to the Pierre Choteau Company. Born in 1858, the son of a Choteau employee, he had been sent to Scotland to be raised and educated. As a young man, however, he returned to the reservation where he hunted, trapped, traded, and guided from his home at Midvale, presently East Glacier Park. *Photo courtesy of Helen Edkins*

*Malenda Wren, interpreter at Old Agency*

Malenda Wren, daughter of Charles Chouquette and his Piegan wife, Rosa Lee, acquired
a good white education. Along with Susie Williams and Isabel Coe, daughter of Joe
Cobell, Malenda was a principal interpreter at Old Agency. *Photo courtesy of Angus Monroe*

*John Bird, Jimmy Grant, Henry Chouquette, and John Night Gun with two young lads, 1895*

Appearing here in a trader's store, probably Joe Kipp's, these men personify a reservation community of Blackfeet, mixed bloods, and whites. *Photo courtesy of Nora Spanish*

*Father Pierre-Jean De Smet with Mr. and Mrs. John Monroe,*
*Mrs. Upham, Mrs. Kipp, and Mrs. Croft*

One of the most famous of the Black Robes was the Jesuit missionary, Father De Smet, called Long Teeth by the Blackfeet, and shown here with some of the more Christian mixed-blood families of the north side of the reservation. *Photo courtesy of Nora Spanish*

*Logging crew from Old Agency, early 1890s, including Mad Wolf (fourth from right)*

To earn extra rations, many Blackfeet joined woodcutting crews or worked at the agency sawmill. Indian labor around the agency became quite common although it was often resented. *Photo courtesy of Sherburne Collection, UM Archives*

## Little Dog, 1890

The growing number of Blackfeet around Old Agency with little to do, their hunger, their need, and the inability of white officials to solve mounting problems, prompted agent John Young to organize a Blackfeet Indian Police in October 1886. Led by Chief Little Dog, head of the Black-Patched-Moccasin Band, many of the twenty members of the force belonged to the men's warrior society, the Mad Dogs, who had long policed the tribe. *Photo courtesy of Nora Spanish*

*White Quiver in horned weasel headdress*

White Quiver, one of the most clever and successful horse raiders in Blackfeet history, was another man of legendary exploits. Confined to the reservation, forced to abandon illegal forays in the closing years of the century, he enrolled with the Indian Police in 1897, hoping to regain the excitement of a warrior's life. *Photo by J. H. Sherburne; courtesy of Sherburne Collection, UM Archives*

*Old Person and wife, with Old Person Number Two (right)*

By the early 1890s a degree of prosperity rewarded the efforts of individual Blackfeet as they began to establish ranches and raise cattle and horses. Cattle offered economic rewards and even greater promise. Pride and a sense of accomplishment returned. The past could be linked to the future and the traditional could find a renewed if limited place. Here, the Old Persons shed their shirts and pants, replacing them for awhile with blankets, necklaces, leggings, and brass-tacked belts. *Photo by Thomas Magee; courtesy of Sherburne Collection, UM Archives*

## Burial grounds at Old Agency

In spite of the whites' presence and their dominating ways, the traditional life survived in bits and pieces. Beloved possessions which accompanied a body in burial now came to include not just a familiar tepee rest, but a rocking chair as well. *Photo by Thomas Magee; courtesy of Sherburne Collection, UM Archives*

## Piegan chiefs

Left to right: Running Crane, White Grass, Four Horns, Brocky, White Calf, young Bear Chief, and Little Plume, with Little Dog seated in front of Brocky.

Photographed in Carlisle, Pennsylvania, in 1892 while in the East to negotiate, these Piegan authorities tried to cope with growing numbers of white prospectors and mining explorations in the mountainous western portion of the reservation. Negotiations for the sale of land concluded in 1895. The Blackfeet received $1,500,000 for their ceded land, retaining rights, however, to hunt, fish, and cut timber there. Once the "ceded strip" opened in 1898, over five hundred prospectors invaded what is now Glacier National Park in the hope of striking it rich. Prominent among these gold seekers were agency employees who had long worked quietly, if not secretly, at finding gold first. There turned out to be little mineral wealth. *Photo by J. N. Choate; courtesy of Smithsonian Institution*

# Social Management:

## *Implanting Reservation Institutions*

THE NEW Blackfeet Agency on Willow Creek represented in its own oblique way a shift in Indian policy and public awareness. The buffalo past, the freedom of an undefined frontier, had been replaced by wooden fence posts set in cadence and strung with wire, by boundary lines, by an orderly peace imposed through law. Whites, convinced that Indians had been given sufficient time for adjustment, determined that the Blackfeet and other Plains warriors would have to conform to the general ordering of the West. A part of that effort at tidying the pioneering mess dictated that plains Indians would be confined to reservations.

The Willow Creek Agency provided an institutional focus for that white perception. Consisting of some twenty-two frame buildings, some with paint and some without, a Government Square, and a ballooning bureaucratic staff, the agency not only spawned an adjacent town, Browning, but it formed an economic magnet in northcentral Montana that proved to be very attractive to outside and white interests.

The new agency developed along lines set down in the 1895 land sale agreement which specified an annual expenditure of $150,000 for the purchase of

*cows, bulls and other stock, goods, clothing, subsistence, agricultural and mechanical implements, in providing employees, in the education of Indian children, procuring medicine and medicinal attendance, in the care and support of the aged, sick, and infirm, and helpless orphans of said Indians, in the erection of such new agency buildings . . . as may be necessary, in assisting the Indians to build houses and enclose their farms and in any other respect to promote their civilization, comfort and improvement.*

Government management of Indian monies with long-term goals made for a new creation — the twentieth century reservation. All Indian reservations were special places if for no other reason than that they were controlled directly by the Indian Service in Washington, D.C., and were exempt from all laws passed by state and local governments. The Blackfeet Reservation was no different. Inside this "special place" the supreme authority was the Indian agent, often referred to in the early years as major, later a superintendent. Others said he was closer to a czar.

Yet if the agent was in command at the local level and unaccountable to local people, he was still held on a short leash by the Indian Service in distant Washington, D.C. Responsible for huge numbers of reports, evaluations, receipts, authorizations, accounts, and slips, the agents became increasingly desk-bound. And they continually enlarged their already expensive staffs to assume the increasing work load.

Indian policy from Washington was often politically shaped and applied without reference to local needs or conditions. The government placed its faith in a systematic institutional approach to specific goals. This faith in organization created the twentieth century reservation, giving it an appearance surprisingly uniform: agency plant, tribal police, boarding schools, missions, licensed traders. This was the reservation, not the land nor the people, but the superimposed institutional apparatus that became so typical.

The reservation's task became one of institutional education, and as one official trenchantly observed, "to educate means breaking up of tribal customs, manners, and barbarious [sic] usages and the assumption of manners, usages and customs of the superior race." The agent, missionary, and schoolmaster soon gave up on the older people, instead concentrating on the children. Indian life could be trained out of them. That replacement of one culture by another was unimaginable as long as the children remained with their families in a traditional setting. Consequently, they were torn away from their families, forced to acquire a new tongue, English, and raised institutionally. Their hair was cropped, they were given ill-fitting clothes and clumsy shoes, and trained to clock and calendar.

By 1907 there were two major boarding schools on the Blackfeet Reservation: Willow Creek, administered by the agency, and the Holy Family Mission school on Two Medicine River. These schools established demonstration farms where the boys could learn how to farm and use implements. In addition to being an "industrial object lesson," these school-run farms provided the foodstuffs for the students and staff and helped financially. Likewise the young girls learned to cut and sew, to do housework, to cook and wash, which also helped the schools be more self-sufficient. Learning was a constant affair — and it had more to do with discipline, short hair, silverware, scrubbing faces and floors, and feeding pigs than with learning nouns, verbs, and common denominators. By 1910 there were 771 children of school age who could attend Holy Family Mission; a day school at the Old Willow Creek complex; the new agency boarding school at Cut Bank Creek; or the off-reservation schools at Fort Shaw, Montana, or Carlisle, in Pennsylvania.

Having to deal with institutions in the form of traders, schools, missions, police, or segments of the agency, in ways that could be measured, catalogued, and managed, pushed all Blackfeet into a white world. Even tribal government was organized into another institution, representative and elective — the Tribal Council. It all was a part of a concerted effort by the federal government to transform warriors into farmers, Indians into whites.

It was a wrenching process; it was also, in spite of family and community, surprisingly successful. The intimacy of the photographic images that follow clearly demonstrate that white modernity arrived via a succession of small and seemingly insignificant things. The acquisitions were often rational enough — boots for moccasins, cotton for hide, sewing machines in place of needles and thread; some came during the hide trade, some later. Yet whatever their origin, however understandable, they possessed unplanned and unwanted repercussions, and all intruded beyond their practical nature. Once these inanimate objects jumped into people's lives their influence could not remain neutral, for their very assumption was an implied, if conditional, promise to greater change.

## Blackfeet Agency, 1911

Completed in 1895, the new Blackfeet Agency on Willow Creek consisted of some twenty-two frame buildings. Agent George Steell reported he required a total of fifty-four agency personnel, including Indian police and judges, and that the agency school employed thirteen full-time teachers. *Photo courtesy of Dorothy McBride*

*Fourth of July Parade, Browning, ca. 1904*

By 1900 the needs of the Willow Creek Agency had outstripped Joe Kipp's trading post and created the town of Browning. While some say it was named after Daniel Browning, the recent Commissioner of Indian Affairs (1895–97), others assert the townsite derived its name from a man called Diamond R. Brown. *Photo by Thomas Magee; courtesy of Don Magee*

*Busy Saturday in front of Sherburne's at Blackfeet Agency, 1899*

A major feature of any Indian agency was the licensed Indian trader. J. H. Sherburne
came to the new agency on Willow Creek in 1895 from the Ponca Reservation in Oklahoma.
Located next to the agency, Sherburne competed with other traders and businessmen,
including Joe Kipp, C. W. Broadwater, and Willits and Scriver, as they all sought to
take advantage of the growing cattle industry and the economic needs of the agency
and the Blackfeet. *Photo by J. H. Sherburne; courtesy of Sherburne Collection, UM Archives*

*Young women inside the Sherburne Mercantile, 1899*

The trading post was a favorite gathering spot where Indians and whites alike could exchange news, gossip, court, look at goods, and buy. As ration days approached, or later when annuity checks were issued on a per capita basis, Indian families from all over the reservation began moving toward the agency and town. Coming to the agency meant coming to the trader. It was a family event. *Courtesy of Sherburne Collection, UM Archives*

*Old Man Running Crane from Northside with George Edwards
(on counter) inside Sherburne store, 1900*

The major activity of the trader, of course, was not to provide a meeting place but rather to sell goods and make a profit. In addition to foodstuffs, the traders sold colored blankets, calico, ribbons, men's clothing, livestock, and farm machinery. They had captive consumers — the Blackfeet — who could not leave the reservation without a permit and who were encouraged and often forced to buy at one of the traders. Big profits were possible in this situation and when the trader extended credit, he would often recover his debt by taking in horses or cattle issued to individual Blackfeet by the government.
*Photo courtesy of Sherburne Collection, UM Archives*

## "Kipp's water system, Blackfeet Agency"

The so-called "Valley of Wild Flowers" on Willow Creek was mainly a problem for the new agency and the townsite. The nearby ground was wet and marshy and the groundwater eroded foundations at the agency and the boarding school. Wells were soon contaminated, posing a continuing health hazard. Drinking water, as a result, had to be hauled in on the railroad and sold in barrels. Kipp's water system was followed by other similar enterprises, including one owned by Green Grass Bull. *Photo courtesy of Oregon Provincial Archives, Society of Jesus, Gonzaga University*

*Judge Running Crane, leader of the Southsiders,
in Army uniform jacket, ca. 1900*

The Indian court with Indian judges was a major feature of the agency. Directed by
dignified leaders who knew their own people and tribal customs, the court worked with
the Indian police to provide better law and order on the reservation than white officials
could. Using their own language, regulating petty affairs and major ones with common
sense and customary law, Blackfeet judges and their court became a significant reservation
institution.

Judge Running Crane was the father of No Coat, also a prominent tribal judge, and
Wades-in-Water, a noted policeman. The Southsiders were the families living south of
Browning. *Photo courtesy of Sherburne Collection, UM Archives*

*Blackfeet policeman, 1902*

The Blackfeet policemen wore distinctive blue cloth uniforms with gold buttons. Provided with separate barracks, uniforms, an oversized six-shooter with a broad leather belt full of shells, and a black hat, these men continued the policing activities of the earlier soldier societies, and struggled to provide order and discipline in the confusion of transition. Settling petty affairs, carrying out orders loyally and impartially, they retained a pride in belonging to an elite group and were recognized as leaders in the Indian community.

*Photo by Thomas Magee; courtesy of Sherburne Collection, UM Archives*

*Arthur E. McFatridge, Superintendent, Blackfeet Agency, 1910–15*

The reservation boundary was strictly controlled after the building of the reservation fence in 1903–4. Indian police manned exit points at Robare, Cut Bank, and Whiskey Gap and passes had to be obtained by Indians wishing to leave or whites wishing to enter. Later, under McFatridge, "Those entering the reservation were required to register at the agency office within twelve hours. Indian police . . . met all trains on horseback. They would see to it that no liquor was brought on the reservation and that all travelers registered in the agency book." *Photo courtesy of Helen Chase and Keith Purtell*

*Superintendent McFatridge's wife and new government car beside the Crow tepee, 1912*

In the Swift Current Valley between Babb and Many Glacier on the western edge of the reservation, the first oil in Montana was discovered in 1906–7. Drilling operations and stock companies were formed by J. H. Sherburne and others who had high hopes. This was also a period of "land allotment," when the government reversed its policy of treating the reservation as the property of the entire tribe. Instead the reservation was to be surveyed and the land "allotted" to individuals in parcels of 40 acres of irrigated land and 280 of grazing, or, if the individual Indian wished, he could take the whole amount of 320 acres in grazing alone. McFatridge concluded the reservation survey in 1912 and, using tribal enrollment statistics, land was allotted to 2,623 Blackfeet to be held in trust by the government. Any unallotted land not required for the towns of Babb and Browning was to be sold under the Enlarged Homestead Act of 1909. *Photo courtesy of Dorothy McBride*

## Government Square, Blackfeet Agency

Agent George Steell upon taking up his position at Willow Creek in 1895 complained that "the location is very bad, as a number of the buildings are located upon mucky, soft ground." Government Square and agency housing had to have an elaborate boardwalk system. *Photo by E. L. Chase; courtesy of Helen Chase and Keith Purtell*

*Tennis court, Browning, ca. 1912*

As the agency grew, it came to include such improbable facilities as this tennis court, built for the enjoyment of white employees but attracting Blackfeet as well. *Photo by E. L. Chase; courtesy of Helen Chase and Keith Purtell*

## Agency slaughterhouse

By 1905 the slaughterhouse at Blackfeet Agency in Browning met growing sanitary concerns and was organized enough to meet the beef needs of the ration rolls. Unlike the earlier slaughter of cattle at Old Agency on Badger Creek, which often had been done outside and with axes Indian fashion, the new agency slaughterhouse conformed to the butchering standards of the government. *Photo by J. H. Sherburne; courtesy of Sherburne Collection, UM Archives*

*Children at old Willow Creek School near Blackfeet Agency, 1907*

From left: Harry Schildt, Josephine Bear Child, B. Connelly, Sam Roundine, George Clark

The dilapidated buildings at Willow Creek, the overcrowding after the boys' dormitory burned in 1897, the poor sanitary conditions, and the health hazards of typhoid from water standing in the basement led the Blackfeet themselves to demand the closing of the Willow Creek School. Washington Inspector Jenkins too urged closing the school, even if it meant sending the children home. W. H. Matson, the superintendent of the school, complained that "an old woodshed, flooded with water when it rains . . . and filled with snow or dirt when it blows in winter, is still used as the boy's bathroom . . . the plaster is falling in places by the foot and by the yard." The facility remained in use until 1909 despite its inadequacies. *Photo by J. H. Sherburne; courtesy of Sherburne Collection, UM Archives*

*Sewing class, Cut Bank Boarding School, 1907*

In spite of their problems, the boarding schools offered children an alternative. Many remembered their time there as the best days of their lives. Mary Ground thought "schools were good. You didn't waste time. They took care of children. . . . The children didn't mind working. They would have had to work at home. The boys brought in the wood and the vegetables. They milked the cows and brought it to the girls who strained it."
*Photo by J. H. Sherburne; courtesy of Sherburne Collection, UM Archives*

*Baking bread at the Willow Creek School, ca. 1907*

Not only did homemaking classes teach skills thought to be necessary for a modern
life, but they supported the daily needs of the boarding school. *Photo by J. H. Sherburne;
courtesy of Sherburne Collection, UM Archives*

*Washing clothes in the school laundry, Willow Creek School, 1907*

In 1902, seven-year-old Tom Many Guns, along with his friend Joe Boss Ribs, went to school. Neither spoke English and Joe wore old blanket pants, but Tom's brothers bought him "some knee pants. We wore knee pants in those days." *Photo by J. H. Sherburne; courtesy of Sherburne Collection, UM Archives*

## Willow Creek mess hall, 1907

Away from their families, their language, their religion, and allowed to visit with parents
only a few times a year, the young Blackfeet were "civilized" by means of soap, scrub
brush, national anthem, short hair, tables, and chairs. *Photo courtesy of Sherburne Collection,*
*UM Archives*

## Cut Bank Boarding School, ca. 1910

Although the boarding schools were an important part of efforts to eradicate the Blackfeet's tribal past, providing the facilities remained a problem. In 1901, for example, 102 children were enrolled at Willow Creek, 70 at Holy Family Mission, 48 at Fort Shaw, and 10 at Carlisle. According to historian Thomas Wessel, that left nearly half of the school-aged children on the reservation without any school. The Cut Bank Boarding School, opened in October 1905, was supposed to handle the overflow. The building plans called for 250 students, yet when finally finished the school facility mysteriously shrank — only 75 could fit — and the deplorable Willow Creek School, which should have been closed, remained in operation. *Photo courtesy of Dorothy McBride*

## Produce and sailor suits

Students about 1912 proudly show off their vegetables raised for the Cut Bank Boarding School. School uniforms were a normal feature of boarding school life, but the popular sailor suits of the era are an odd touch on the inland prairie. *Photo by E. L. Chase; courtesy of Helen Chase and Keith Purtell*

## Browning Day School, 1913–14

The Browning Day School, opened in 1905, was a public school essentially for children who actually lived in Browning or at the agency itself. *Photo by E. L. Chase; courtesy of Helen Chase and Keith Purtell*

*Fort Shaw girls' basketball team, 1901*

The industrial school at Fort Shaw, Montana, like all the off-reservation boarding schools, placed a great deal of emphasis upon sports. Here the Fort Shaw girls' basketball team of 1901 poses after a winning season. *Photo courtesy of Don Magee*

*James Bad Marriage running around end, Fort Shaw, ca. 1915*

Although strict and often drab, the boarding schools had lighter moments when sports, music, or just young spirits relieved the homesickness, the strain of speaking English, and the discipline of taskmasters. *Photo courtesy of Montana Historical Society*

## Delegation of Piegan Indians to Washington, D.C., 1891

Left to right, seated: Four Horns, Little Bear, Running Crane, Little Dog, and Little Plume. Standing: White Calf, George Steell (Agent), Brocky or Tail Feathers Coming Over the Hill, Shorty White Grass, and Joe Kipp (trader).

White Calf and the traditional headmen of the various Piegan bands made up an informal "tribal council" which was often used by reservation agents to gain compliance with agency policy. After George Steell took charge of Old Agency in 1890, he deliberately challenged the authority of Chief White Calf and the other headmen. "Put each man," he reported, "on equal footing and the influence of the chiefs and medicine men will disappear." Since, however, negotiations for the "ceded strip" in 1895, ration reductions, cattle issues, and tribal enrollment matters all required some form of representation on the part of the tribe, the council was consulted — reluctantly perhaps — but consulted nonetheless. *Photo courtesy of Smithsonian Institution*

*Delegation of 1903 to Washington, D.C.*

Standing, left to right: Owl Child, Joe Tatsey, Little Bear Chief, Four Horns, Zack Miller, and Mountain Chief. Seated, left to right: Bill Russell, Little Dog, and Curly Bear.

Following the death of White Calf in 1903, the Blackfeet Tribal Council became more structured and attempted to assume a more independent authority. Growing political and economic differences between mixed and full bloods contributed to this shift, as did the dissatisfaction of the more aggressive, more prosperous mixed bloods with traditional forms of tribal authority. The growing influence of the council also represented another attempt on the part of agency officials to transform an informal, traditional function into a structured, bureaucratic one.

In cases such as this one of 1903, delegations of local people or of the council itself traveled to Washington, D.C., to provide information on the Blackfeet independent of the local agent or to plead for special consideration with the Commissioner of Indian Affairs. *Photo by D. L. Gill; courtesy of UM Archives*

*Blackfeet Tribal Council, ca. 1909*

Standing from left to right: Black Weasel, Wolf Plume, Split Ears, Billy Kipp, Dick Sanderville, Jim Perrine, No Coat, Joe Brown, Owl Child, Charley Buck, unidentified, Malcolm Clarke, Running Crane. Sitting, left to right: Curly Bear, Bear Chief, Chief Crow, Little Dog, Bull Calf, and Mountain Chief.

The economic issues and the matter of who legally belonged to the tribe caused great unrest among the mixed bloods who numerically prevailed. With the possible phasing out of the reservation through the allotment process, the economic stakes and the role and composition of the tribal council became critical. Superintendents could no longer ignore the council after 1910; they repeatedly attempted to bully it or appoint those Blackfeet who supported them. Often they were men like James Perrine, Levi Burd, Stuart Hazlett, Malcolm Clarke, Charles Buck, and Zack Miller, mixed-blood men who spoke English well and who were alert to their individual economic interests rather than tribal ones. *Photo by E. L. Chase; courtesy of Helen Chase and Keith Purtell*

# The Sun Dance:

## *Tradition as Inspiration*

As LATE as 1900, the outward trappings of Anglo-Christian culture had not obscured Blackfeet traditional culture. Periodically, often through tribal celebrations, the culture revealed its continued strength. The most sacred of these Blackfeet ceremonies was the Sun Dance, observed when the prairie grass was greenest, when the cow parsnip was at its highest, on the warm days of early summer. The bands, scattered throughout the reservation, slowly drifted together to form a great circle camp. Each band, whether Hard-Top-Knots, Fat Melters, Worm People, or Skunks, took up its time-honored place in a great circle. After three days of detailed, careful preparation, the Blackfeet build a medicine lodge dedicated to the sun, the source of all power. Centered within the tribal circle, this "Okan," roofed with willows and festooned with offerings, became a sacred place of powerful prayer, sacrifice, and spiritual renewal for the collected Blackfeet.

A mother, grandmother, aunt, or wife initiated this most sacred celebration of renewal either to overcome the threat of danger or sickness to a loved one or as an expression of gratitude for having survived some dramatic peril. In either case she pledged or "vowed" to the sun to assume the demanding responsibilities required in sponsoring a dance dedicated to the sun. The "vow woman" had to have led a pure life. She had to carefully, properly, prepare the sacred food — buffalo or beef tongues — for those joining her in her pledge. She also had to learn intricate prayer sequences, to purchase a sacred headdress and other "power" articles, to fast, and to provide the focus for a tribal celebration of social and religious significance. A vow to the sun worked a real and definite hardship. It was not undertaken lightly. It was expensive. There were repercussions, drastic and supernatural, for shortcomings and mistakes, intentional or not. In their sacrifice, a single family came to shoulder a tribal obligation that reached out to an awe inspiring power, the holy sun.

By the beginning of the twentieth century, influenced by white efforts to discourage their "heathen worship, the painting of faces, and the beating of tom-toms," the Blackfeet moved the midsummer Sun Dance to coincide with the patriotic white celebration of the birth of the United States — the Fourth of July. Somehow, continuing the Blackfeet religious and cultural life under the guise of a national holiday with American flags, ice cream, and parades made the preservation of tribal traditions more acceptable in the eyes of the Indian Service.

The Fourth of July Sun Dance gathering became a major tourist event as well. Setting aside their "civilized clothes," leaving their frame or log houses, individual Blackfeet again became the "noble redmen" of their warrior past and the Sun Dance became a photographic event with mock battles, horse races, gambling, singing, and dancing along with the more important events of reverent sacrifice, "medicine," and prayer. For adult Blackfeet the Sun Dance was an opportunity to revive and to teach, through example, an ethical system and a threatened history. For homesteading whites and city tourists, it was an entry into a world that was simply exotic.

Ignoring changes in their own dress, overlooking many of the subtle compromises reservation life demanded as well as the tourists with Kodaks, Blackfeet people continued to celebrate their traditions, their belief in the sun, and in themselves. This reaffirmation offered particular solace for the cultural homesickness the Blackfeet encountered.

Blackfeet persistence and success at cultural survival so infuriated local agents, missionaries, and reformers in general that they asserted that the greatest single obstacle to civilizing the Blackfeet was the Sun Dance on July 4. With increasing irritation these whites dedicated themselves in print and in action to forcing its abandonment. In 1910, after four decades of Catholic missionary work among the Blackfeet, J. B. Carroll, S.J., became so incensed with the endurance of Indian values via the Fourth of July that he wrote a vituperative article entitled "The Fourth of July Dishonored" for the *Indian Sentinel.* This diatribe is a wonderfully descriptive document by an intelligent, informed, bigoted, and frustrated observer. Advancing from erroneous premises and for all the wrong reasons, Father Carroll inadvertently, yet correctly, analyzes for us the significance of the Sun Dance to the reservation Blackfeet.

Carroll begins by rhetorically asking why it is that the Fourth of July is the greatest day of the year on the reservation, more important than Easter and Christmas rolled into one. He quickly concludes:

*not because of our free institutions and national greatness, but because it reminds them of the darkest days of heathenism and bloodshed, because it is the day on which they parade as real savages in their war paints and war dances. . . .*

What Carroll is saying, of course, is that the Blackfeet had become Indians again. Warriors from the past returned to a timeless rhythm of tradition and event that left them re-created in their contemporary world. Now transformed, Carroll goes on:

*They think themselves wise, and in their conceit they are satisfied with themselves, imagining that their ways are as good for Indians as white people's ways are for white people.*

Such a transformation Carroll and others found deplorable and said so, repeatedly.

Not only does Carroll point out that the Blackfeet "think that their old heathen customs are just as good as civilized customs, and even more venerable" but he forcefully and derisively describes the sacred character and intensity of their devotion to them. "Thus it is," he writes, *that the Indians call the Fourth of July Umnarkatvik-sistsikui, i.e., Big Holy Day, because it is on this day above all other days that they celebrate their holy medicine, holy drumming, holy howling and dancing, their holy painting and dressing . . . with holy skins and furs and leathers and bells, and many other "holy" things.*

Carroll was right. The complex Sun Dance celebration exuded a sense of sanctity and although he denigrated it, he clearly recognized the power of such a cultural and spiritual experience. Carroll also correctly saw the Sun Dance as a major obstacle to "civilizing and Christianizing" the Blackfeet. It reinforced former ways. Preserving honor, allowing the emergence of suppressed dignity, the sacred cycle bridged the past while giving both past and present a positive value. Being Indian meant something far different than that which had become everyday — dusty overalls, too large a bill at the trader's, and too many hours at a dreary farm job, or even worse, nothing to do.

Carroll accurately reflected reservation reality when he observed that Blackfeet pride in their own values and customs was sufficiently objectionable without trainloads of whites streaming off the platform at Browning while others converged by wagon to view the medicine lodge. "The Indians," he wrote, "must be greatly confirmed in the idea that their holy medicine is powerful. . . . Armed with cameras and umbrellas and seeking invitations, whites are foolish enough to admire and encourage such diabolical abominations." In frustration, Carroll concludes: "So, what should be the Indians' shame becomes their glory, and they become more desperately settled in the darkness of barbarism."

The Blackfeet Sun Dance affirmed in a series of sacred acts, sacrifice, and vision, an annual renewal — one that gave the Blackfeet enough presence and strength to go on for another year. Such a cycle could not be denied, however abbreviated or altered. Past momentarily became present and the history the Blackfeet claimed became aspiration.

## Sun Dance camp, Browning, July 1900

Spreading out on the Willow Creek plain west of the agency, the bands set up their 273 lodges with the medicine lodge in the center. The painted tepees of the headmen occupy prominent, designated positions on the inner circle. Clustered behind, their followers erected their lodges in equally traditional sequences. *Photo courtesy of Sherburne Collection, UM Archives*

*"Rainbow Lodge"*

Tepees painted with individual designs and symbolic decorations were never numerous if for no other reason than that they were expensive and demanding. These special lodges with their holy or "power" symbols were acquired through dreams, visions, or exceptional personal experiences that were touched by "grace." Whoever discovered these "power signs" owned them; when placed on their tepees, the signs suffused those lodges and their occupants with protective power. On the tepee pictured above, a man is holding a pipe which he is filling to give the sun a smoke; he is also offering eagle tail feathers.
*Photo by J. H. Sherburne; courtesy of Sherburne Collection, UM Archives*

## "Bear Chief's War Lodge"

These powerful, personal tepees had their own identity and it was questionable who owned whom — did Medicine Owl possess the Snake Tepee or did it possess him? In spite of this ambiguity, power tepees could be transferred, passed on to family heirs or sold, much as medicine bundles or pipes. Ownership brought authority and prestige, but it also carried onerous responsibilities as well. Public ceremonies had to be sponsored; restrictive taboos had to be observed; certain words could not be uttered; gifts had to be given; prayers had to be said. *Photo by J. H. Sherburne; courtesy of Sherburne Collection, UM Archives*

*Mountain Chief and his wife with wooden horse effigy*
*outside his Otter Tepee at encampment*

Celebrated horse raiders often carried carved, wooden horse effigies while dancing and recounting their military exploits. At a grass dance some years earlier Mountain Chief, according to Walter McClintock in his *Old Indian Trails,* held "a stick which represented a horse. He crossed the circle and handed it to a visiting Sioux Indian." *Photo by Kiser; courtesy of Gary Schmautz*

*Blackfeet women, ca. 1900*

In fashions typical of early reservation life, these imposing ladies wear a variety of headdresses as they prepare for the coming medicine lodge. *Photo by Kiser; courtesy of Sherburne Collection, UM Archives*

*Elk Horn, the camp crier*

A member of the Fat Melters band and the men's warrior society, the Mad Dogs, Elk Horn, tall and forceful, commanded respect as he announced events or assignments. *Photo by Walter McClintock; courtesy of Glacier National Park Archives*

*"Receiving the offering for the sun"*

*Photo by J. H. Sherburne; courtesy of Sherburne Collection, UM Archives*

## Vow woman and attendants

These virtuous women, weak from fasting, proceed slowly with great solemnity to the medicine lodge. The vow woman, head down in reverence, wears the sacred headdress contained in the "natoas" or Sun Dance bundle. *Photo by J. H. Sherburne; courtesy of Sherburne Collection, UM Archives*

*"Coming to the lodge after a three-day fast"*

Mrs. Big Nose is led by the medicine man Bull Child in his famous robe.

*Photo courtesy of Sherburne Collection, UM Archives*

*Medicine men with sacred buffalo skull in front of sweat lodge,
ca. 1900*

While the "vow woman" fasted and prayed, the men prepared themselves for the coming
medicine lodge ceremony by erecting sweat houses composed of one hundred willows
and then covered the willows with hides. Purifying themselves in the smoke of sweetgrass,
these men, probably from the men's warrior society, the Mad Dogs, pose for their picture.
*Photo by Thomas Magee; courtesy of Don Magee*

## Sham battle, 1899

Piegans and visitors acted out war exploits and victories of former days by firing rifles, shouting, singing war songs, and counting "coup," both on horseback and off. These reenactments, sometimes called "horse-dancing," drew appreciative audiences. Many of the older warriors had experienced the intertribal warfare, the horse stealing raids, and they used this opportunity to remind all present of Blackfeet heroism. Later, with the gradual disappearance of the older warriors, the sham battles no longer reflected a reality of Blackfeet life and increasingly became an element of their disconnected past. *Photo by Thomas Magee; courtesy of Sherburne Collection, UM Archives*

## Raising the medicine lodge, 1911

Knowledgeable medicine men selected the site of the medicine lodge, dug the holes for the cottonwood posts that would be its foundation, and guided the camp as it selected cottonwoods and willows from a nearby creek bottom. It took a full morning of hard work by the young men of the bands to gather up the necessary trees, branches, and green boughs. Having hauled the cottonwood logs to the camp, the Blackfeet began construction by setting upright nine to twelve cottonwood posts, forked at the top. They then laid horizontal logs in the notches of those posts, forming an eight-sided circle about nine feet off the ground. Later, log rafters running from the center post would rest on top of the foundation. *Photo courtesy of Dorothy McBride*

## Raising the center pole

A war party scouted out the center pole for the medicine lodge. An outstanding warrior was chosen to fell a large cottonwood tree with a red-bladed ax. With great ceremony, the war band fired their guns into the "enemy pole" and then, after it crashed to earth, "counted coup" on it by breaking off its branches.

After the pole was hauled back to camp, the next stage occurred as sunset approached. Strong young men from the various bands and societies lined up in four separate lines like spokes of a wheel — north, south, east, and west — as the sun slowly dropped over the mountains to the west. Holding long poles tied together at the top with rawhide thongs, the men sang the old ceremonial song as they stamped slowly forward. Then, having converged, suddenly they attacked the enemy pole, hoisting it up with ropes. It was dangerous work. Cradling the rafters, they lifted them, too, bridging the gap between center pole and the outside perimeter of the medicine lodge. *Photo by Walter McClintock; courtesy of Glacier National Park Archives*

## Blackfeet raising medicine lodge, 1910

Men and women wait expectantly for the rafters to be lashed to the center pole. The rawhide lashing has just been cut by a renowned warrior in a ceremony called "the cutting of the hide." Beginning from the tail of a green beef hide, the honored fighter cuts one looping circle after another until he has cut a single long thong. The honored hide cutter and his relatives had to make many gifts of horses, blankets, and clothes.

Once the framework was erected and lashed together, tribal gifts and offerings were tied to the small end of the stringers that stuck out beyond the center pole. *Photo by Thomas Magee; courtesy of Don Magee*

*Three Bears relating how he had killed an enemy warrior*

Three Bears had been selected because of his bravery to cut the green hide in strips to tie the rafters to the outside frame and center pole. As he did so, he stopped to tell of his many exploits, pointing out and relating details. *Photo by Walter McClintock; courtesy of Glacier National Park Archives*

## Bringing in the willows

The final phase in the construction of the medicine lodge was the covering of the sides of the lodge the morning after the raising of the center pole. Here the Crazy Dogs (Mad Dogs), a men's warrior society, bring in the sacred one hundred willows. Singing, shooting, and shouting accompanied the laying of the willow boughs against the framework. The medicine lodge was complete. Four days of ceremony had passed. *Photo by Walter McClintock; courtesy of Glacier National Park Archives*

## Offerings in the medicine lodge, July 1899

Offerings of blankets or colorful material fluttered at the top of the center pole whose function was to tie heaven and earth together in a cosmic whole. *Photo by Thomas Magee; courtesy of Sherburne Collection, UM Archives*

## In the medicine lodge, ca. 1910

Warriors in the medicine lodge sit in a semicircle around the center pole, which has offerings of blankets tied to it and guns resting against it. The man in the foreground is digging a fire pit in which "coup sticks" will be burned as the various warriors act out their war exploits with shouting, gestures, and shooting. *Photo by Walter Shelley Phillips; courtesy of University of Washington Library*

*Medicine men blowing eagle bone whistles from the weather booth*

Left to right: Spotted Eagle, Chief Elk, and Bull Child

Inside the medicine lodge, opposite the entrance, a special booth of willows housed the weather dancers, who fasted and prayed there. These medicine or holy men had enough spiritual power to influence the elements — to drive away rain, to divide or gather clouds, to make cold weather. The Blackfeet expected the weather dancers to use their charms, paints, incantations, and dances to bless them with "sun power." People with vows, offerings, and gifts came to the booth to have their faces painted and to have these holy men pray for them that "they might be endowed with power." *Photo courtesy of University of Washington Archives*

## The Doves at the encampment, ca. 1910

The Doves, or Pigeons, a young men's warrior society, perform their special society dance. Jumping with both feet together in their peculiar way, arrows and bows pointed down, they recount their exploits and exaggerate their bravery as they seek to inspire themselves and others.

These age-grade warrior societies were common. In addition to the Doves there were Mosquitoes, Kit Foxes, Brave Dogs, and others. Made up of the members of many bands, these societies got together at the sun dance to feast, to dance, to police, and to hunt.

Standing at far right is Fish Wolf Robe in beaded vest and armbands, while Stabs-Down-By-Mistake, with elaborate breast plate, dances in the middle and Little Dog glances to his left. *Photo courtesy of Nora Spanish*

*Black Bull (left) and Stabs-Down-By-Mistake
with drum at Sun Dance encampment, ca. 1900*

*Photo courtesy of Joe Bear Medicine*

**89  The Sun Dance:** *Tradition as Inspiration*

*Blackfeet medicine lodge dance with Mike Shortman leading the Crazy Dogs, July 4, 1907*

The Stars and Stripes are everywhere, but especially visible on the dancer near the right end of the line wearing what resembles a dunce hat. *Photo by Thomas Magee; courtesy of Don Magee*

*Medicine lodge at 1911 Sun Dance with Superintendent
McFatridge (arms folded) and unknown white visitor in center*

*Photo by J. H. Sherburne; courtesy of Sherburne Collection, Montana Archives*

*White Quiver (left foreground) and Jack Big Moon (far right),*
*Willow Creek, ca. 1900*

White Quiver is wearing his medicine headdress, war shirt, and leggings, Big Moon an ermine-trimmed war shirt and leggings. *Photo courtesy of Sherburne Collection, UM Archives*

*Grass dancers of Black Horse society led by Tom Medicine Bull*

The grass dance was imported by the Blackfeet from the Assiniboine — often called Hair Parters because of their hair style. The dancers imitated the manner of the prairie chicken during mating season. Bobbing and weaving from side to side to the steady rhythm, making a pecking motion with their heads, these well-outfitted dancers inspired others and enjoyed their opportunity to wear old-time Indian dress. *Photo by Thomas Magee; courtesy of Don Magee*

*Drummers inside the medicine lodge, July 1900,*
*with interested onlookers*

*Photo by J. H. Sherburne; courtesy of Sherburne Collection, UM Archives*

## Calf Shirt, 1898

Calf Shirt was a Blood Indian whose medicine, or sacred helper, was the rattlesnake. Carrying his rattlesnakes with him until his death shortly after 1900, Calf Shirt doctored various ailments. Famous with the Bloods and the Piegans, he often appeared with his live snakes to demonstrate his medicine at the various dances and encampments. *Photo by Thomas Magee; courtesy of Don Magee*

## Calf Tail giving a name

During the medicine lodge ceremony, Calf Tail (standing) is about to give the man in front of him a name — a newer, better, and more significant name. With this name he will be shoved into the world to make his way. *Photo by Thomas Magee; courtesy of Don Magee*

# Getting By:

## *The Economics of Survival*

After 1900, despite the tremendous development of the homesteading frontier beyond the reservation to the east and south, and despite huge investment in cattle and irrigation projects, the economic condition of Blackfeet people deteriorated.

The old debate on how best to provide an economic base for the Blackfeet surfaced again and again. The Indian Office in Washington, D.C., and the local agents, even when well-intentioned, could not agree on a strategy for development. Two basic positions emerged, each with a solid block of supporters. One approach emphasized grazing and saw in stock-raising — cattle for Chicago and horses for Montana homesteaders — a realistic hope for the Blackfeet to become self-employed and self-sufficient. The other maintained that the responsibility of both the Indian Office and the agent in Browning was not just to make "their wards" economically independent, but "to civilize" them — to force acculturation and assimilation into Christian, white society. Farming seemed a more appropriate way to achieve these added goals. Farming required a discipline of time and effort and encouraged values that could only be described as more virtuous, more responsible, and therefore more civilizing than stock-raising.

Reservation conditions often remained divorced from the simmering bureaucratic debate, which was conducted within the Indian Office in Washington, D.C., in correspondence to and from senatorial offices, and on the agency grounds in Browning. Local inspection unfortunately played a minor role in determining priorities; nor were the Blackfeet themselves united on the best use of their resources. Both sides attempted to win the proponents of irrigation to their cause — expensive irrigation projects were begun either to expand hay production beyond the naturally watered meadows or to allow the development of truck farms and vegetable gardens. Irrigation systems, however, simply did not attract the Indian use or support that white officials anticipated.

George Bird Grinnell and Special Agent Edgar A. Allen, along with other agents and inspectors familiar with the reservation — its high, windy plains, its abrupt weather, its discouraging summer frosts — thought the discussion a ridiculous one. Commercial farming, however ennobling, had no place, they felt. This was livestock country. If the Blackfeet were to translate their labor into economic salvation, they could only trigger this transformation by raising and selling livestock. As to the civilizing responsibilities of the Indian Office and the Browning agent, first things first — first meet the economic need, then worry about the debilitating effects of being cowboys. In the early years, the ranching proponents prevailed.

Following the devastating winter of 1886–87 the very nature of the area's cattle industry underwent radical change. Open-range grazing was too risky. Ranch farming to produce hay crops for winter feed was the response, and this meant more water to irrigate hayfields. The Blackfeet Reservation possessed water in great abundance. St. Mary's River, Two Medicine River, Birch Creek, Badger Creek, Willow Creek, Cut Bank Creek — all tumbled out east of the Rockies and irrigated Blackfeet grass. It was an undulating dream.

Many agents, beginning with John Catlin in 1890, recognized this and urged the government to use Blackfeet money to develop the cattle industry. One stock issue followed another; agency farmers schooled the Blackfeet on the fine art of making hay, erecting sheds, and breeding selectively. By the beginning of the new century over 9,000 head of Blackfeet cattle marked a profitable stock-raising enterprise. The arrival of the Great Northern in 1895 had connected the Blackfeet to Chicago, and newly developed irrigation systems on Willow Creek provided ample hay crops.

Serious problems remained, however. Not many Blackfeet were involved in the emerging cattle industry. By 1902 only 572 out of an Indian population of over 2,000 possessed any cattle at all. The cattle issues aimed at giving each individual Indian a stake in utilizing the expansive grazing potential of tribal lands, but this democratic procedure of per capita distribution did not ensure widespread ownership. Whites who had married into the tribe, mixed bloods, agency traders, and a few enterprising full bloods quickly came to own most of the tribal cattle roaming the reservation. By trading for horses or rations, and by settling bad debts at the traders or bar bills at Dupuyer, too many Blackfeet quickly lost the cattle they had been issued. As Thomas Wessel, a historian for the U.S. Indian Claims Commission, noted: "Full bloods in particular did not care — they did what they had been trained to do since childhood when not at war or on the hunt. They moved around the reservation relating past deeds of valor to set an example for a future generation of warriors."

Cattle trespass also threatened the Blackfeet livestock effort. Blackfeet grassland seemed an oasis — so much so that in 1904 one Indian Service inspector estimated that between 8,000 and 10,000 cattle were trespassing. Many bore the brand of the Flowerree Cattle Company or of William G. Conrad. If the Blackfeet cattle industry was to survive, it had to be protected from such encroachment. Many people, particularly Blackfeet cattlemen, came to believe that the only solution was to build a fence around the reservation. Even Agent James Monteath pushed for the rapid construction of a boundary fence.

When the reservation was finally fenced in 1904 — at Blackfeet expense — it did little good. No sooner was the fence completed than mysterious outbreaks of fence-cutting surfaced. Pressure on the Blackfeet grasslands was increased by the droughts of 1904 and 1905, which made the reservation even more attractive to neighboring white ranchers. The Indian Office in Washington, in spite of the violent objections of the Blackfeet Tribal Council, responded by opening up the reservation to white grazing through a permit system. Once again, when it counted, there was little choice. Political influence still prevailed with the Indian Service and the rudimentary Indian economic base, resting upon scarce, nutritious grass, was further diminished.

The long tough winter of 1906–7 only worsened the problem. Winter feed became scarce. Disease, so often attendant with drought, swept the reservation herds. The cumbersome permit system and the presence of large herds of diseased cattle from off the reservation inflicted even more severe damage on Indian stock. The situation depressed many Blackfeet, particularly the full bloods. A few decided to shift from raising cattle to horses; others wanted to give up stock-raising altogether.

Having failed to provide the Indian cattle industry with the help it needed, the Indian Office and Agent Monteath abandoned it for another program. A congressional order alotting land to individual Indians in 1907 dealt another blow to stock raising and marked the beginning of an elaborate program of diversified farming. The new approach incorporated the decade's most cherished beliefs about irrigation, the family farm, and individual self-sufficiency. Monteath also hoped irrigation would provide for quicker results and greater employment than ranching. Confiding in Commissioner of Indian Service W. A. Jones, he said he would create work thereby terminating rations and even annuity goods. This reduction would be accomplished through a wholehearted commitment to irrigation and farming while stock-raising would become a side issue.

The general enthusiasm for irrigation on the Great Plains evidently overwhelmed the agency staff and Agent Monteath. The Blackfeet, they reasoned, could become self-sufficient farmers if they took advantage of modern technology and irrigation. With the western mountains of the reservation watering Badger Creek, Cut Bank Creek, the Two Medicine and Milk rivers, agriculture had to be the answer. Besides, in addition to bringing rewards, farming encouraged the "right attitudes"; it would remove the Blackfeet from the baffling fluctuations of a cattle market for which they were educationally unprepared and it would lump them into colonies of suspendered, hard-working farmers where they could be more easily supervised, regulated, and directed. There was nothing malicious about the concept as far as agency officials were concerned. Along with many others of the period they shared the belief that farming was a better activity than cowboying. As one historian put it: "Agriculture stood to land as cooking did to raw meat. It converted nature into culture. Uncultivated land meant uncultivated men."

This assumption that farming equaled a school transforming savages to citizens underlay other official ideas. Only colonies of farmers, some argued, could answer the continuing economic problems on the reservation. Colonies would allow greater supervision, communal use of equipment, and less duplication of services. Blackfeet resources could be used more efficiently and more effectively. The real targets in this "New Policy" were the full bloods, those traditional Indians who had not prospered and who filled the ration rolls.

Yet irrigation, in spite of its tremendous expense in capital and labor, did not work. Renewed efforts, more engineering studies, greater cost, and continued employment could not prevent the failure. Government inspectors reviewing plans or maintenance costs remained dubious about the projects and individual Piegans often rejected them, refusing to farm their irrigated acreage or preferring grazing allotments.

Attempting to rationalize previous commitment, to salvage something of the gigantic expense involved, new evaluations argued that irrigation had never been designed for intensive farming in the first place. These were limited systems, designed only to supplement the cattle industry by watering hay meadows for winter feed. Moreover, construction on the various irrigation projects had kept many full bloods employed as laborers and, given the limited job opportunities, such employment had benefited the tribe. Elderly Blackfeet often confirmed this contention. Payday was reason enough to support government irrigation projects. Something was better than nothing.

Meanwhile, the cattle industry continued to regress. It was, as the preeminent historian of the Blackfeet, John Ewers, phrased it in his book *The Blackfeet: Raiders on the Northwestern Plains,* "a failure, even during the few years it was a financial success." Outside of Browning, beyond the immediacy of the agency, there was little attention or instruction given to Indian ranchers.

Even though cattle prices climbed for a short time prior to and during World War I, few Indians profited except by the sale of horses to homesteaders who had taken up claims south and east of the reservation. With free land a mania, and convinced that they could "dryland" farm, these settlers needed huge numbers of horses to break sod and turn it upside down in long furrows. J. H. Sherburne, astute economic wizard and licensed trader, reported years later that the Blackfeet Reservation became "the center of sales to many horse buyers and individuals who came for the purpose of buying stock for the farming operations."

Yet whether farming, selling horses, or raising beef, the Blackfeet found that success remained partial and terribly uncertain. A part of the problem was the lack of a single, consistently articulated policy. Ten different superintendents reigned in their wainscoted quarters between 1905 and 1921, stamping documents and writing reports defending their actions. Tenure for some lasted but one or two months, particularly after 1915; some agents were corrupt and dismissed from the Indian Service for embezzlement of tribal funds and property. Others were too willing to tolerate negligence, drinking, or bouts of self-interest among the agency staff. Although a degree of bureaucratic ineptitude if not corruption had long been a fact of reservation life, after 1910 it reached alarming proportions, adding its demoralizing presence to an already discouraging set of economic and natural obstacles.

The debate over which economic approach to take, stock-raising or farming, had created various alliances among the Blackfeet, and they attempted whenever possible to enter the discussions, which were usually set in the superintendent's office. Policies, personalities, and corruption all overlapped, creating a situation in which there was no neutral ground. Each new appointment made the new man, involuntarily, a member of a debating society in which positions had already been taken and fought over. Past decisions and failures prevented each new agent from aspiring to continuity; instead each man had to predict what the new economic times would be like and whether the government solution would be to encourage a tribal or an individual approach, one that relied upon stock-raising or farming. Each solution had its ranks of supporters and detractors among the outspoken reservation factions and, because of the collapsing cattle industry, each side conspired to reach a new dispensation.

While the economic debate on the reservation seesawed between 1905 and 1921, the rest of Montana, particularly the east slope of the Rockies, had experienced a massive influx of homesteaders. Attracted by the generous legislation of the Homestead Acts of 1909 and 1912; the reclamation projects on the Milk River, the Sun River, and the lower Yellowstone; and a boisterous promotional campaign by the Great Northern, the Northern Pacific, and the Milwaukee railroad companies, farmers flooded across the vast, flat, semiarid plains. Arriving in boxcars and fanning out from Ingomar, Big Sandy, and Dutton, these homesteaders brought an abundance of hope, youth, muscle, and determination. Some 90,000 homesteaders filed at the land offices in Great Falls and Miles City between 1905 and 1919; while the wet cycle on the Great Plains lasted they performed wonders — so much so that the government constantly held them up as an example of what the reservation could be: a checkerboard of farming property. Yet that property was fragile; it depended upon moisture, upon rainfall, and after more than ten years of exceptional wetness, the dry cycle of less-than-normal moisture returned. It began in north central Montana in 1917; by 1918 it intensified and spread south and east. In 1919 all of Montana hosted a devastating drought. With the heat, the dryness, came range fires, grasshoppers, clacking, whirling Mormon crickets that devoured everything from wheat to leather hinges. There were other plagues — cutworms, wireworms, smut — and the blowing winds scattered thistle and topsoil. Grain and cattle prices plummeted after the war in Europe ended. The booming agricultural world of the homesteader collapsed, strangling towns, closing banks, and bringing foreclosures.

The long, harsh winters followed by summers of continuing drought brought farming, dryland or otherwise, to a standstill. Settlement could not be maintained. Thousands streamed out of Montana in a mass exodus, vacating in the process years of numbing dawn to dark labor, homes, and an altered landscape.

The Blackfeet, however, could not leave. Bound to an original homeland, anchored to individual acreages that had been allotted in 1907, they stayed where they had always been and faced the same economic depression, the same fateful combination of winter and drought as their neighbors beyond the reservation fence, the same pattern of foreclosure on the allotted land they held in fee simple. Only here the foreclosing was done mainly by licensed reservation traders — W. C. Broadwater and J. H. Sherburne.

Already weakened by years of clashing policies, bureaucratic ineptness, and the growing rivalry between full bloods and mixed bloods, the Blackfeet were reduced by the drought years of 1917–20 to poverty, sickness, hunger, and malnutrition. By 1919–20 two-thirds of the entire tribal population of some 3,000 relied upon government rations. Something had to be done. Once again the Indian Office responded by appointing a new agent. This time it was Fred C. Campbell, an energetic veteran of the Indian Service and an experienced stockman familiar with the reservation and northern Montana. Amid rumors of starvation among the full bloods at Heart Butte and along Cut Bank Creek, Superintendent Campbell conducted a thorough, house-to-house survey to learn conditions firsthand and to demonstrate that the government cared.

After careful investigation Campbell concluded that the cattle industry was a terrible failure for all but a few enterprising mixed bloods. If the Blackfeet were to experience relief, it would have to come in the form of self-help. Individuals must plant gardens, grow a bit of grain, and raise a few head of stock along with chickens and pigs. Individual self-sufficiency, not tribal efforts, was the key that would prevent starvation, relieve the government ration rolls, and open the future.

Straddling the old arguments, Campbell initiated a Five-Year Program that relied upon Indian effort. The program, designated the Piegan Farming and Livestock Association, had over twenty-five district chapters across the reservation. Coming after years of drought, Campbell had little difficulty in convincing the Blackfeet that water and irrigation were essential whether they farmed or raised stock. Campbell aimed his program at the full blood population, and it elicited criticism from other tribal members who wanted a greater commitment to cattle. In fact, the farming and livestock chapters, although imparting a sense of purpose, did little to alter the overall Blackfeet condition.

Nor did the arrival in 1929 of Campbell's successor, Forrest Stone, improve the effort at self-sufficiency. Superintendent Stone's contribution consisted in yet another turn in the zigzag pattern of economic development. This time it was sheep. Stone became convinced that the reservation's economic future during the Depression years of the early 1930s rested on the acceptable profit margins of sheep and wool. The continuing governmental financial crisis of the 1930s, however, soon curtailed the agency's effort. The next plan was to bring sheep in from the outside. The range had improved with increased moisture in the 1920s and the early 1930s, and Oregon and Washington sheepmen would pay substantial grazing fees, bringing income to the Blackfeet without investment and without work. The permit system was revived and it worked well, but not for the Blackfeet. It left them without range, without work, without future prospect. It was another economic dead end.

In the years prior to World War II the situation remained essentially static. Some efforts in the late thirties and early forties aimed at reinvigorating the cattle business; a few succeeded. Gas and oil, first discovered on reservation land at the turn of the century, but only recently in demand, provided a little income from nonagricultural sources. None of this was enough. The reservation community, fractured as always between the interests of the declining full bloods and the opportunistic mixed bloods, experienced a depression greater than other Montanans. At least the others could leave. The Blackfeet could not.

Stuck on their reservation without employment and failed by a government which had declared itself responsible for guiding them to economic independence, the Blackfeet languished. Despite the expenditure of millions of dollars of Blackfeet money and fifty years of Indian Service activity, little had changed since 1886. The reservation and its institutions had failed. When the 1940s began, the Blackfeet were as dependent a people as they had been following the end of the buffalo.

*"Cowboys and saddle ponies in camp on the range," ca. 1890s*

An awesome amount of well-watered grassland made the Blackfeet Reservation prime grazing land. Most Blackfeet favored ranching over farming, and the Blackfeet cattle industry prospered until after the century turned. But so too did white trespassers — cattle barons like Dan Floweree, who illegally grazed their immense herds on Blackfeet land in such numbers as to comprise an "invasion." Many young Blackfeet men turned to cowboying for the big outfits. *Photo by Barker; courtesy of UM Archives*

*Elijah Jeff Devereaux and his daughter Spyna*

Like Hugh Monroe, Elijah Jeff Devereaux was typical of the white adventurer on the make. Originally from Maine and the sawmills of Minnesota, he followed the mining camps from Virginia City to Blackfoot City, traded horses, freighted and raised stock at Fort Benton, and finally joined the whiskey traders north of the Medicine Line, where he survived the Cypress Hills Massacre. About 1889 he settled down on his wife's Indian allotment on Cut Bank River to raise cattle on a large scale. *Photo courtesy of Lottie Bond*

## Henry Devereaux, Sam Bird, Tom Aubrey, ca. 1910

Elijah's son Henry posed with Sam Bird and Tom Aubrey, the first mayor of Browning.
These men epitomized the Blackfeet cattle industry. They were mixed bloods — more
aggressive, better educated members of the reservation community who found cattle a
rewarding investment and Indian land an available commodity. *Photo courtesy of Lottie Bond*

*Lomie Goss and John Mountain Chief horse-pulling in front of Sherburne store, 1907*

Horse-pulling contests were a popular reservation pastime at the turn of the century among the many cowboys and ranchers. Horse-pulling generated the same betting enthusiasm as horse racing. *Photo by J. L. Sherburne; courtesy of Sherburne Collection, UM Archives*

*Dipping vats on the Duck Lake road at the old Percival place*

The Indian Office belatedly provided these dipping vats to help combat mange and other infections in the tribal herd and in the private stock of Indian cattlemen. Mange outbreaks became particularly acute when trespassing white-owned cattle infected the Indian herds after 1900. *Photo courtesy of Lottie Bond*

*Using "slip scraper" in construction of St. Mary's Canal near Babb, 1908*

In 1907, as part of the first Blackfeet allotment act, Congress appropriated $100,000 to construct irrigation ditches. Competent and enterprising Indians needed water, it was argued, to become profitable farmers on their individual allotments. The U.S. Reclamation Service linked St. Mary's Lake to the Milk River and engineered less ambitious projects on Two Medicine River, Willow Creek, and Cut Bank Creek. Tribal money and loans paid for construction and maintenance of the ditches and numerous Blackfeet were employed on the projects. *Photo by J. L. Sherburne; courtesy of Sherburne Collection, UM Archives*

*Hanging out the wash at Spotted Bear's place on Big Badger,
Heart Butte, ca. 1920*

In 1919 agricultural depression hit all of Montana, brought on by extreme drought,
plummeting grain and cattle prices, bank failures, and farm foreclosures. Thousands of
homesteaders fled. The Blackfeet could not. Bound to their allotments, they stayed to
face drought, depression, and near starvation. Many Blackfeet were forced to sell their
newly allotted land at a loss or saw it foreclosed by licensed reservation traders.

The "longhairs" in the full-blood communities such as Heart Butte withdrew to their
traditional homes and survived — usually on less than their mixed-blood relatives. *Photo
courtesy of Fred Des Rosier*

*Peter and Orcelia Flintsmoker, Under Beaver Flintsmoker,
and Martha Spearson in front of their house*

The Indian Office solution to all problems was to appoint a new agent. This time it
was Fred C. Campbell, an energetic veteran of the Indian Service and an experienced
Montana stockman. Amid swirling rumors of starvation among the full bloods like the
Flintsmokers, Superintendent Campbell conducted house-to-house surveys to learn of
conditions firsthand.

Campbell concluded that relief could only come through a program of Indian self-
help. Individual Indians and their families would have to plant gardens, grow a bit of
grain, raise a few head of stock along with chickens and pigs. Only then would there
be relief. *Photo courtesy of Fred Des Rosier*

*Piegan Farming and Livestock Association,*
*White Grass Chapter, ca. 1924*

Members include, back row fourth from right: John Ground, Mike Takes Gun, Paul White Grass, Short Face, Juniper Old Person. Others include Charlie and Mark Mad Wolf, Old Mad Wolf, Many Hides, Rosie Mad Wolf, Minnie Dusty Bull, Stehakee.

Agent Campbell felt that the future for at least the full bloods rested with small-scale agriculture. No one would starve. He organized the reservation into a farming and livestock association with twenty-seven chapters and named this self-help plan a "Five-Year Industrial Program." Campbell's opponents, led by such mixed bloods as Robert Hamilton, labeled him a Bolshevik. *Photo courtesy of Rose Tatsey*

*Heart Butte graduates, first Five-Year Industrial Program, 1921*

The Heart Butte district with its large number of full bloods was the focus of Campbell's efforts. There, 92 of 120 families attempted to garden and farm, and there the program achieved its greatest success. The chapters produced 126,000 pounds of potatoes, 5,000 pounds of carrots, 16,000 pounds of rutabagas, and other garden vegetables, and in so doing prevented a recurrence of the near starvation of 1920. *Photo courtesy of Jim Reevis*

*Albert Mad Plume, wife Susan, son Fred, and granddaughter Irene with vegetables from their garden*

The Mad Plumes were typical of full bloods in the late 1920s who supported Superintendent Fred Campbell's efforts to develop self-sufficiency. *Photo courtesy of Mae Vallance*

*Split Ears with bounty string of three thousand gopher tails, 1920*

Drought, gophers, wire worms, cattle mange, and Mormon crickets all played devastating parts in the collapse of the Blackfeet ranching and homesteading economy. An important element of Campbell's program for Blackfeet recovery centered on ridding the reservation of gophers. A bounty of ten cents per tail gave many Indians an opportunity to earn a little cash. *Photo courtesy of Peter Red Horn*

## Harvesting wheat, ca. 1920

The Blackfeet agricultural chapters produced enough wheat — 15,000 bushels by 1922, the second year of the program — that Campbell constructed a flour mill in the Heart Butte district and requested funding for another. *Photo courtesy of Peter Red Horn*

*Owen and Rosa Heavy Breast with hay crop at their ranch*

Owen Heavy Breast, born in 1879, was one of the more successful full-blood wheat ranchers. Here, he and his wife stand with their hay crop to demonstrate their success, the fertility of the soil, and the promise farming held for the Blackfeet. *Photo courtesy of Glacier National Park Archives*

## Midwinter Fair, Browning High School gym, 1920s

The celebrated Midwinter Fair at the Browning school gymnasium provided detailed
instruction in farming techniques as well as an opportunity to show off the past year's
achievements. With needlework exhibits, canning demonstrations, quilting bees, and
traditional craft displays, the fair became a community event supporting Agent Campbell's
contention that self-help through agriculture was the solution to Blackfeet economic
problems.

## Instruction in raising wheat, Midwinter Fair

Government instructors at the winter fair gave useful advice and information to attentive Blackfeet: when to begin spring planting; when and where the men could get grass, grain, and garden seed; what machinery was necessary, and where they could get it from the government or from one of their neighbors. *Photo courtesy of Montana Historical Society*

## Albert Mad Plume and family

By 1922 the Five-Year Industrial Program expanded to include livestock. Superintendent Campbell wanted to issue milk cows, sheep, chickens, and pigs to those who had demonstrated their ability to manage crops, land, and machinery. *Photo courtesy of Fred Des Rosier*

*Superintendent Fred C. Campbell and Heart Butte farmers*

Standing, from left to right: unidentified, Joe Bull Shoe, White Quiver, Fred Campbell, No Coat, Buffalo Body, Good Gun. Sitting: Richard Sanderville, unidentified, Melvin D. Strong

Frequent visits, encouragement, and instruction by the superintendent kept up Blackfeet interest and involvement in the Five-Year Program. Moreover, the success in putting food on the table was real and of immediate benefit. *Photo courtesy of Rose Tatsey*

## Lewis Plenty Treaties (Bear Child)

Plenty Treaties supported the Five-Year Industrial Program. *Photo courtesy of Peter Red Horn*

*Dedication of oil well, ca. 1928*

By 1921 oil leases were another feature of the reservation. The Blackfeet Tribal Council promoted oil investment to provide employment and to relieve the general poverty of the tribe. But the council often differed with the Department of Interior on how best to protect the interests of the Blackfeet. Oil leases and the question of control of the Blackfeet tribal resources became a major issue of the late 1920s. *Photo courtesy of Peter Red Horn*

## Alex Marceau and grandmother

As the 1920s drew to a close, there was some improvement in the living conditions of the Blackfeet. Whatever the shortcomings of Campbell's program, no one starved, the ration rolls were reduced, and home conditions improved. *Photo courtesy of Marceau family*

*Jason and Bob Salway in front of Reim house, 1921*

Agriculture did not eliminate ranching, as these two cowboys attest. But even among the more established ranchers north of Browning, the emphasis had changed. *Photo courtesy of Lottie Bond*

*Shrine convention, June 27, 1923, Washington, D.C.*

Left to right: unidentified, unidentified, White Quiver, Charley Reevis, Levi Burd, Bird Rattler, boy, and Victor J. Evans, with Two Guns White Calf on far right

Criticism by Robert Hamilton and James Willard Schultz, noted author of *My Life As an Indian* and numerous adventure tales, that the Blackfeet were starving under Campbell's leadership prompted the agent to arrange for thirty-five selected full bloods, members of the Piegan farming and livestock chapters, to attend a Shrine convention and tour Washington, D.C. *Photo courtesy of UM Archives*

*Digging water lines, 1934, Blackfeet Agency*

Like millions of other Americans, the Blackfeet welcomed government relief programs
in the 1930s. Building bridges, digging water mains, constructing roads, New Deal public
work projects such as Civilian Conservation Corps/Indian Agency provided needed
employment on the reservation. These federal programs drastically increased the
importance of the town of Browning and the dependence of the Blackfeet upon the
federal government. *Photo courtesy of Sherburne Collection, UM Archives*

## Logging crew, CCC/Indian Agency, Browning

In addition to other public projects, the CCC/Indian Agency was involved in reforestation and logging operations on the western side of the reservation, adjacent to Glacier National Park. *Photo courtesy of Sherburne Collection, UM Archives*

*Moonlight school at Little Badger, 1932*

This Heart Butte group was enrolled in the "moonlight school," in an effort to eradicate illiteracy. Organized in 1932 by Forrest Stone, superintendent of the Blackfeet Reservation, and Douglas Gold, the superintendent of Browning Public Schools, the clinics enlisted rural schoolteachers to teach older Blackfeet people to read and write English. *Photo courtesy of Mae Vallance*

*Tom Spotted Eagle, Old Red Head, and Jim Spotted Eagle demonstrate their reading ability in front of Heart Butte Round Hall*

Adults attended school in two-hour periods. Interest was reported as good. In many cases children and grandchildren of the older participants did the interpreting. Everyone made some progress: they added new words to their vocabulary, managed to write beginning sentences, and all learned in some measure to read. In the process the adults discovered how necessary it was for their children to go to school regularly. *Photo courtesy of Fred Des Rosier*

*Moonlight school at Browning*

Here, older Blackfeet demonstrate their newly acquired reading ability.

*Photo by Elliott Studio, Whitefish; courtesy of Mae Vallance*

*John Little Blaze, No Coat, and Sure Chief making baskets at Heart Butte Round Hall, 1932*

Although the Blackfeet had no basket-making tradition, one of the moonlight school instructors, Mae Vallance, showed the men how, and it came to be a masculine diversion for some during the Depression years when little was going on. *Photo courtesy of Fred Des Rosier*

## Mrs. Wolf Plume and Good Victory Spotted Eagle

During the ten-minute recesses, men and women hauled out sacks of tobacco, smoked, and talked. Lunches were often served by the "bean patrol," who marshaled out the portions. *Photo by Mae Vallance; courtesy of Mae Vallance*

*Tom Dog Gun, Aloysius Evans, and Sam Calf Robe with easels
at Heart Butte, 1932*

Painting was another craft taught at the moonlight schools in the make-work atmosphere
of the time. *Photo courtesy of Mae Vallance*

*W.P.A. sewing club from Two Medicine*

Left to right: Mrs. Calf Looking, Mae Williamson, Nora Spanish, Louise Pepion, Tiny Racine, Anna Potts, Rosy Big Beaver

New programs brought efforts to improve housing, hygiene, and education. Women played an important role in this goal, naturally, and many craft groups such as this one were formed. *Photo by Olga Ross Hannon; courtesy of MSU Archives*

*Little Badger Women's Club, ca. 1933*

*Photo by Mae Vallance; courtesy of Mae Vallance*

*Blackfeet craft clubs from Starr School, Old Agency, Browning,
and Two Medicine in front of craft shop, Browning, 1929*

*Photo courtesy of MSU Special Collections*

*Stabs-Down-By-Mistake addressing the Tribal Council, with*
*White Calf and Rides-at-the-Door to the right looking on, 1930s*

*Photo by Helen M. Post; courtesy of UM Archives*

# A Diminished Way of Life:

## *Changes in Tradition*

AMERICANS RECOGNIZED that the twentieth century had brought sweeping change and innovation. The world of the western frontier had slipped away, and Americans basked in nostalgia. The "vanishing American" became a cliche for much of this fond romanticism. Indian people, however, seemed unaware of their sentimental, romantic role. The Blackfeet, for example, instead of slipping away, actually increased in number while adapting to a white world that was itself experiencing conflict and tension, insecurity and a disquieting impermanence. The result was a strange collision on the reservation — growing numbers of Blackfeet, growing poverty, clashing traditions, and yet numbing inactivity. Reservation institutions did not extinguish the Blackfeet nor their culture; they did, however, diminish them, forcing replacement of certain aspects of their culture, modifying their lives in bewildering ways.

The result was colossal change. Wagons replaced travois, log cabins and wall tents took the place of tepees, black suit clothes were substituted for buckskin, and hats were shaped to declare "Indianness." Indian life was more and more affected by white material goods, legal considerations, manners, and language. Was this conversion or realistic adaptation? Were these natural first steps toward acculturation or simply convenient, more efficient ways of doing "Indian" things? It was hard to tell. Young kids in short-clipped hair could sit patiently at school desks, fathers could wear Prince Albert coats and gold watches, mothers in aprons could push strollers across the dry prairie. They were still Blackfeet, yet choices were unavoidable and the external trappings mirrored internal changes. How much could individual Blackfeet change and yet remain Indian? No one was certain.

The contrasts and contradictions in the following photographs are but an indication of how the wall of the past gradually thickened, further alienating the present from the past. What had been to most Blackfeet adults a constant, if unformulated, awareness changed its shape into memory or, worse yet, was simply forgotten. Periodically a trapdoor opened into that memory and a whiff of half-forgotten scents or a glimpse of the old world escaped. The greater part of reservation life, however, was spent on the everyday level of getting up and going to bed in an increasingly white, English-speaking world. Finding work, keeping it, avoiding it; putting food and meals on the table, keeping warm and getting sick; sending kids to boarding school, staying out of trouble, or hauling water; it was everyday life that mattered and it was the same and yet not the same.

There were alternations between excitement and tedium, between being Indian and acting white.

Too often when whites intervened in this reservation world it was as government officials administering to their wards, as missionaries Christianizing, or as individual men hoping to use their marriages to Blackfeet women to profit from tribal grazing rights. Others, such as traders, came to prove the superiority of their culture or to take economic advantage. White and Indian worlds overlapped. Seldom did they fuse. Too often the gulf remained, widened by an imperfectly concealed air of white superiority or abysmal indifference. To the Indians it was the same thing. They were Blackfeet and yet they were no longer whole. Now seams crossed their lives, stitching together activities, events, decisions, and choices. The result was not enhancing, for the seams were like boundaries and frontiers — they had to be crossed and recrossed and there were so many.

Fragmenting and dividing experiences and private lives, the reservation brought an awareness to the Blackfeet that somehow things were fractured and disjointed. Living with cattle, sheep, and chickens, with gardens, cars, and money, with umbrellas, iron cookstoves, and wheels, required countless adjustments and reactions. There was no premeditated cultural betrayal yet the white world intruded more and more. Everywhere individuals faced choices and the impact of those choices made for new sensibilities and new indifferences. It was for the Blackfeet the tiny, quiet things that brought revolution. It was almost a secret how lives could become different, yet still be Indian. There were no conspicuous discoveries made in loud proclamations by the leading elders or a camp herald. Choices, instead, were often obscured if not hidden. If someone recognized now and again what had transpired or saw portents in their "medicine," they spoke only in Blackfeet and to a very few.

Although growing in numbers, the Blackfeet found themselves increasingly diminished. They were not, however, just victims. Tenaciously they hung on to what they had, the reservation, its isolation, and to themselves. They ingeniously converted white practices to Indian sensibilities — vests came to be beaded in wondrous floral patterns; American flags appeared on moccasins and cradleboards; Shriner pennants flapped in the breeze atop tepee poles; and machine-made oriental carpets covered sweat lodges and lined tepees. Things did change, but they also remained surprisingly similar.

Reservation life, then, replaced the old space, the old sequences in time, and it initiated a silent, gradual unraveling. Certainly the reservation minimized the shock of survival, but just as certainly it forced alterations in individual lives. The push of reservation life became increasingly public, surrounded by relatives, friends, and enemies. It was a life in which envy was a well-understood emotion. The struggle in this close-knit world allowed for no neutral ground. The encroaching world closed in and all the more effectively because now the reservation had a boundary that had to be leaned on; a separation that had to be vivid to be believed. It was unnerving. In the process of choice the Blackfeet as a whole became poorer in spirit and recognizably, indisputably, "reservation."

## Peddling buffalo horns

Shortly after the completion of the Great Northern in 1895, Blackfeet men often sold buffalo horns to tourists alongside the railroad tracks. *Photo courtesy of Public Archives of Canada*

*George Bird Grinnell with informants*
*in front of the Sherburne Mercantile*

Anthropologists became a common feature of reservation life as they made annual trips
west to study the Piegan. *Photo courtesy of UM Archives*

*Canvas tepees with wagons along the Lower St. Mary's Lake, ca. 1911*

Reservation life had changed the Blackfeet by 1900. There were alterations both subtle and drastic. Wagons had replaced most travois; cabins or wall tents replaced tepees, or at least were favored in the wintertime. *Photo courtesy of Sherburne Collection, UM Archives*

*Piegan camp in January, ca. 1915*

*Photo by H. F. Robinson; courtesy of Museum of New Mexico*

## Woman and travois during winter of 1898

The photographer noted: "An infant was packed into the bundle on the travois — and when the woman saw me taking the picture she leaned over the baby and turned her back to prevent getting the baby's picture as he peeked out of the pack." This photo was taken at the present location of the Browning Mercantile. *Photo by J. H. Sherburne; courtesy of Sherburne Collection, UM Archives*

*Tanning hides adjacent to the Otter tepee, ca. 1915*

Not all traditional activities were abandoned. Yet new associations, new situations, new ways of doing the old tasks came to possess a growing, if not overwhelming, appeal.
*Photo by H. F. Robinson; courtesy of Museum of New Mexico*

## Elk Horn and son, ca. 1900

Elk Horn was the principal camp herald at many of the Sun Dance encampments at
the turn of the century as well as a leader of the Grease Melters. *Photo by Thomas Magee;
courtesy of Angelo Greco*

## No Coat and daughter, July 1899

Proud parents were often interested in having their portraits taken with their children. Many photographs of this kind document the Blackfeet's continued interest in a traditional past. *Photo by Thomas Magee; courtesy of Don Magee*

*Brothers No Coat and Wades-in-Water and their wives in 1899*

A reservation dress made up of a mixture of white and Indian elements emerged very early. Blankets, calico dresses, vests ornamented with pocket watches and fobs — all take their place in a traditional environment and all register the mounting changes for Blackfeet men and women. *Photo by Thomas Magee; courtesy of Angelo Greco*

*"Old Lady Juneau," mother of Dennis and Emily, who was married to Barney Boss Ribs of Heart Butte*

The Otter tepee shown here with Mrs. Juneau was not only made of canvas, but it was painted with a broad brush and commercial paints. Its "medicine" or spiritual power, however, remained intact despite the external changes and so did "Old Lady Juneau."
*Photo by Thomas Magee; courtesy of Don Magee*

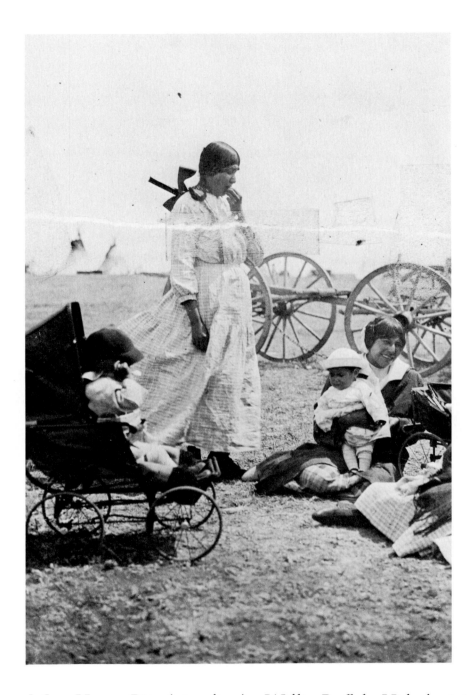

*Mrs. Harry Bite* (standing)*, Willie Buffalo Hides's sister, and their children during a summer encampment, ca. 1910*

Baby buggies, sailor caps, pointed lace-up shoes, and patterned dresses contrast with wagon wheels and tepees. *Photo courtesy of Mrs. Vielle*

*Family portrait at Sun Dance encampment with a prized*
*possession — a Singer sewing machine — ca. 1908*

The advent of cloth dresses, calico men's shirts, and sewn canvas tepees encouraged
Blackfeet women to learn to sew on a treadle Singer and to decorate their dresses with
brass thimbles. *Photo by Thomas Magee; courtesy of Don Magee*

*Early dance hall with young Blackfeet men performing, ca. 1900*

From left: Wades-in-Water, Split Ears, unidentified, unidentified, Irving Little Plume, Elk Horn, Charles Reevis, Little Owl, unidentified, War Bonnet, Big Brave's Son

Change came to the Grass Dancers too. They moved inside and danced under bunting, flags, and kerosene light rather than the open sky. Yet the dance did not change. The elaborate dress remained essentially the same with roaches, cloth shirts, feather bustles, bells, and brass-tacked belts. The sense of being linked to the past, of tradition and continuity, remained. *Photo by J. H. Sherburne; courtesy of Albert Parolini*

*Portrait of Lame Bear (left) and unknown man*

Reservation dress in 1906 included the distinctive hats, vests, and trousers worn by Lame Bear here on the left. Why his friend on the right is wearing two pairs of pants is more mysterious. The photographer's studio posed real identity problems for young people.
*Photo by Thomas Magee; courtesy of Sherburne Collection, UM Archives*

## Four Horns, ca. 1908

Resplendent in Prince Albert coat, white shirt, beautifully tied tie, and dangling gold watch, Four Horns stares at the camera in fierce dignity. If he felt uncomfortable in this "getup," he certainly did not show it. *Photo by Thomas Magee; courtesy of Sherburne Collection, UM Archives*

## Curly Bear, 1912

Insignia, including a Woodrow Wilson campaign button, helped relieve the drabness of the white man's clothes. *Photo by Walter Shelley Phillips; courtesy of University of Washington Library*

*The Coat with his wife, Broken Leg Coat, and Ida Oscar (left)*
*at Cut Bank Creek*

Photo by Thomas Magee; courtesy of Don Magee

*Pete and Maggie Marceau and baby*

Differences in dress, in degree of accommodation, in hair style, reflected individual choices and individual circumstances. *Photo by N. F. Forsyth; courtesy of Elizabeth Lewis*

## Three generations of Blackfeet women

Old Lady Guardipee stands on the left, Agnes Guardipee Augare on the right, while Little Otter Woman, wife of Running Crane and mother of Mrs. Guardipee, sits with eyes closed. The three generations of women reflect three stages of dress, from the most traditional to white linen with contrasting belt and shoes. *Photo by Thomas Magee; courtesy of Don Magee*

## Bostwick children dressed for church

A brother and sister dressed for church in their very best. While moccasins might have been more in keeping with the girl's traditional dress, brass-tacked belt, and Indian doll, her mother, Mary Bostwick, a full blood married to Frank Bostwick, thought lace-up shoes were more durable. *Photo courtesy of Sherburne Collection, UM Archives*

*Blackfeet family with husband in "civilian" clothing*

On the reservation "civilian" meant in the white man's style, and therefore in the agency's eyes more desirable. *Photo courtesy of Rose Tatsey*

## Mother and daughter

Mothers passed on their clothing traditions to their daughters: dress patterns, hair styles, thimbles, and belts. But change still marked the generations. Here, the daughter sports stockings, lace-up shoes — on the reservation an emphatic mark of "civilization" — and shortened dress. *Photo by Thomas Magee; courtesy of Don Magee*

*Joe Calf Robe* (*left*) *and others, ca. 1910*

The man with his back turned carries the Otter medicine bundle, while the children pose in suits, bow-ties, and knickers. *Photo by Thomas Magee; courtesy of Don Magee*

*Mother and children at Sun Dance encampment, ca. 1910*

*Photo courtesy of Joe Bear Medicine*

*Camp life during 1928 Sun Dance*

Clustering together with families, horses, and wagons, the Blackfeet returned to traditional life (if not traditional dress) for a few days. *Photo courtesy of Peter Marceau, Sr.*

*Hauling firewood for the ever-present wood stove*

*Photo courtesy of Joe Bear Medicine*

*Charles White Swan, Dick Lucero, Gambler, January 15, 1912*

The photographer's studio presented certain difficulties. How would you show yourself: as a dandy with laced shoes, tie, and bowler hat; a conservative with work boots, corduroy pants, and short hair; or a traditional Indian with blanket, braids, reservation hat, and moccasins? These three men made their choices clear. *Photo courtesy of Nora Spanish*

*Charley De Roche, his wife Julia Wolftail De Roche, and family*

Benjamin sits next to his father, Annie on her mother's lap; other children unidentified.

This family characterized the changing nature of the reservation as Blackfeet and white traditions merged. *Photo courtesy of Ida Bremner*

*Frank Harrison and Pipe Woman, 1900*

Mixed marriages were common as a reservation community of full bloods, mixed bloods, and whites emerged around the turn of the century. *Photo courtesy of UM Archives*

# Blackfeet in a Modern World:
## *The Past Remains*

THE Blackfeet journey outward across the cultural frontiers lengthened after the Great Depression of the 1930s, leading to further transformations large and small. Many of these changes had been set in motion at the turn of the century with the creation of the reservation, only to reach their conclusion some forty years later. Full bloods declined to a distinct minority and language slipped away; most reservation residents gave up or gave way to circumstances and tried to earn a living by working in what had been a foreign way — official work for the government, teaching school, driving off the reservation to work seasonally fighting fire, picking sugar beets, and haying. There was social change and often economic improvement, although many Blackfeet were still trapped in poverty and joblessness. Circumstances could be as relentless as they were brutal.

Young adults began to look for new ways to live. They wanted somehow to change the patterns of the elderly, to be transported to something different and better. From the very start, they were self-conscious about what they were doing. There was tension and antagonism with the parents and elders who did not understand why the young people reached for acceptance, for comfort, and for employment.

Young people were pleased with their progress and yet, as Blackfeet, many recognized their strange new condition. They had grown up hearing Blackfeet spoken, had seen the "Doves" dance, had listened to the old men "count coup" in the Sun Dance Lodge — yet now they were speaking only English, listening to national radio shows, buying pickups and hay balers and joining the Marines. But change meant opportunity, and although once in a while there would be a nagging twinge of regret at leaving behind traditional Indian life, usually individuals were too busy learning to fix carburetors and brake drums or ferrying kids to school. When the opportunity presented, some individual families moved to different parts of the reservation; others migrated from the traditional locations on Two Medicine River or Badger Creek to Browning where the action seemed to be. They wanted to get away. The old, the traditional, restricted. Yet when away, those who left family, place, friends encountered the old problem of identity. Something important had been left behind. It was not just language, not just long-braids tied with flannel, nor was it just missing friends and the old family ways of celebrating mystery. It had to do with cultivating a life, piecing together a personality that was in striking contrast to the poor, often befuddled, exile, the full blood living out his years as best he could in cloudy mixtures of memory.

By the 1940s the fathers and mothers of the century before had dwindled to a minority; usually it was easier for them to survive than for their culture. Still, through the mid-1940s the traditional Sun Dance continued; women made their vows and gathered their sacrifices, while men made gallant efforts to stay the same. Both consciously tried to carry on traditionally. Small, isolated clusters at Heart Butte, Starr School, and Birch Creek deliberately stuck to the old ways, avoiding whenever possible the contamination of Browning. It was small-scale work though, and while many among the reservation community applauded this effort at traditional life by the full bloods, others found such separateness irritating, an obstacle in fact to tribal progress.

It is difficult now to enter the circle of Blackfeet debate then. There were no written programs, no published theories on how to define "Indianness" or what the Blackfeet approach to contemporary life should be. Certainly there was criticism and conflict between tribal factions as to how problems ought to be addressed. Certainly full bloods and mixed bloods tried to expose each other's self-interest on tribal matters having to do with agriculture, cattle, irrigation, and Bureau of Indian Affairs' governance. Yet this was essentially an internal debate and a verbal one — it is hard to get at now. This much seems clear, however: instead of centering on how to continue or complete a historical culture that came close to being severed, attention focused on daily, pragmatic, individual issues. With the exception of Robert Hamilton working in the 1920s, there was no one among the Blackfeet themselves who seemed to be promising a conscious, systematic design for the tribal task of survival.

The desire to lead "normal" lives in northern Montana did not mean the emotional abandonment of the past, however vague and slippery Blackfeet identity may have become. There may have been no Blackfeet prophets, no over-arching ideological design, but there were honest, sincere, individual attempts at keeping the cultural inheritance alive. This was not done out of a sense of preserving a set of traditions that were dying. It was done because, without pretense and self-consciousness, it felt right, because it needed to be, not because Blackfeet individuals needed to *become* Indians through religious and cultural activities, but because they *were* Indians. Cutting and hauling the sacred willows for the medicine lodge, weather-dancing, singing the pole hymn, Blackfeet elders continued to celebrate themselves and their past in meaningful ways. The past remained — abbreviated perhaps, but still potent, still shaping the liquid present.

This abbreviated past continued beyond World War II, the end of this photographic study, in much the same pragmatic way. The war years of intertribal raiding, the early reservation experiences of band survival, and the former cultural vitality receded a bit further. More changes intruded, changing what home looked like and what it was. The Tribal Council led the growing reservation population through the fifties and sixties, through ever-increasing complexity. Photographically, however, that journey is a very different one than the one we have traced.

After World War II cameras and film changed, and so, too, did photographers and motives, so much so that a sharp division split the photographic record. Miniature cameras became a craze. Everyone wanted a 35 mm camera that could be held to the eye, that would allow rapid fire "shooting," that could be carried easily, that would be "handy." Color photographs, first slides and then prints, Kodachrome and Kodacolor, overwhelmed American sensibilities. The older, larger, black and white format seemed old-fashioned, dull, and worst of all unrealistic. Slide shows became popular social gatherings and Leica, Pentax, and Instamatic became household words.

The photographers themselves changed as well. White tourists no longer thought that Indians were so exotic once outward appearance had changed. Now they spoke English (and often well), went to college, practiced demanding professions, and worked driving school buses and baling hay behind John Deeres like everyone else. Their Indian character remained but it was more personal, more interior, possessing a more private dimension and one that could not be measured photographically. The cultural survivals were no longer paraded for outsiders at tourist events but now were cautiously guarded. The Blackfeet as a consequence appeared "too normal" to require documentation, and white photographers turned instead to the splendid scenery of Glacier National Park.

Left alone, the Blackfeet became their own photographers. Going to war in the 1940s meant enlisting and fighting; it entailed working in the shipyards at Bremerton; and it exposed many to a life beyond the reservation. Many left the reservation forever, coming back only for holidays, for deaths, for family occasions. The reservation no longer was the same. Those who returned and those who stayed began with their new exposure, their new confidence, and their new prosperity to take their own pictures and snapshots. Cameras were hauled out from jockey boxes, dresser drawers, and camp tents for weddings, parades, and picnics. Japanese 35s, Instamatics, and Polaroids recorded not so much tribal life as family and individual passages. Albums were started, added to, and then finished with enough enthusiasm to start another. And on the tops of TV sets photographs in frames both simple and elaborate stood in zigzag lines. There was a recent high school graduate in color, the last picture of grandma at Indian Days, and pushed to the back in faded grey was father in his Marine Corps uniform just in front of the yellow-fringed pillow case of John F. Kennedy. In other living rooms it was an eagle wing fan that hung over the photographs that decorated a sideboard in an intimate corner available only for the close inspection of family members. These photographs in their selection and adjustable arrangement resembled a house altar or shrine binding together the living and the dead. They reminded family members who they were and why they were, and they reached down to veins of feeling that lay deep beneath the surface.

The Blackfeet preserved in this new photographic world represent another reservation people. There is continuity to be sure, but it is deeper, more private, and more interior. The new photographic record is as Indian as before but greater decoding efforts are required and it needs to be done by the Blackfeet themselves. That is another book, theirs and not mine.

*Singing at the Sun Dance Encampment, Browning, 1943*

Foreground, left to right: Frank Choate, Bill Shoot, Turtle, Mud Head, Tom Spotted Eagle

Traditional life continued, centering on the religious ceremonies associated with the Sun Dance. It was difficult, however, to retain the interest of younger people, particularly as the language slipped away. *Photo by Olga Ross Hannon; courtesy of MSU Special Collections*

*Praying and burning the sweet grass, Little Badger, July 1, 1945*

In front of the skull and the sweat lodge three women, including the vow woman, lean over their parfleche containing the sacred tongues. *Photo by Olga Ross Hannon; courtesy of MSU Special Collections*

*Hauling the hundred willows and center pole for the medicine lodge
from Cut Bank Creek to Browning, ca. 1935*

Photo courtesy of Elmer Parolini

*Standing and singing the center pole song, Browning, 1937*

*Photo courtesy of Elmer Parolini*

*Mrs. Wolf Plume, Strikes First (left), and Mrs. Heavy Runner (right) attend the vow woman at Little Badger Sun Dance, 1943*

Proceeding slowly, reverently, these women approach the medicine lodge, wearing ceremonial dresses of deer and antelope skins. *Photo by Olga Ross Hannon; courtesy of MSU Special Collections*

*Weathermen Three Calf and Chewing Black Bones in their
weather booth, Sun Dance encampment, July 1944*

*Photo courtesy of Elmer Parolini*

*Women parading during Sun Dance celebration, 1940*

*Courtesy of Sherburne Collection, UM Archives*

*Short Face and Turtle (both with arms folded)*
*playing stick game, 1938*

Photo courtesy of Elmer Parolini

*Putting up painted tepee on a windy day, Browning, 1939*

Photo courtesy of MSU Special Collections

*Little Blaze and his wife Snakes-in-the-Grass painting tepee cover
with old-style brush, ca. 1930s*

*Photo courtesy of Mrs. Vielle*

181  Blackfeet in a Modern World: *The Past Remains*

## Chief All Over and his son George

Chief All Over is shown here in his Hudson's Bay blanket capote and eagle-tail fan. The All Over family lived over the gap, south of Heart Butte. *Photo courtesy of Elizabeth Lewis*

*Medicine Smoke ceremony, Browning, 1940s*

John Bear Medicine is second from right, with drum. The medicine bundle in front of him is the Crow bundle. *Photo courtesy of Joe Bear Medicine*

*Blackfeet girls at tuberculosis sanitarium, Lapwai, Idaho, 1930*

Left to right: Ella Edwards, Flora Bremner, Alice Walters, Florence Guardipee, unidentified, unidentified, Laura Walters Jamison, Bea Paul. *Photo courtesy of Peter Red Horn*

*Old timers in best of finery*

Left to right: Mountain Chief, Bad Marriage, Bird Rattler, Medicine Boss Ribs, Middle Rider, Fish Wolf Robe. *Photo courtesy of UM Archives*

*Old timers in front of Mint Saloon in Browning watching the street traffic, ca. 1940s*

Left to right: Mike Bad Old Man, Eddie Double Runner, John Mountain Chief, Good Gun, Arrow Top Knot, Rides-at-the-Door, Lazy Boy, Black Weasel, Green Grass Bull, and Jim White Calf. *Photo courtesy of Sherburne Collection, UM Archives*

# "So That's What It Was Like":

# *The Blackfeet and Their Photographers*

THE LONG TRADITION of Blackfeet picture-writing, with its shorthand portrayal of war actions, was one attempt at getting at the question, "What was it like?" Photography was another. By 1888, after George Eastman had developed a simple, handy camera, growing numbers of both part-time and professional photographers worked to capture examples of life on Montana's rapidly passing frontier. Armed with "magic boxes" and a sense that the Western landscape was changing, they recorded as painters had earlier done images they knew to be fleeting. Photographers seemed pushed by a shouldering, insistent sense of urgency. The last moment was now. This general, last-minute rush to document visually the ambiguities of swift, rushing change sometimes included the Blackfeet and their reservation life on those rolling Northern Plains.

The camera's "magic" was surprising and curious. Stopping action, freezing a constantly swirling, interconnected world into small, manageable pieces, the camera recorded. Reality could be held not only between the eyes, but magically between the fingers. It could be examined, preserved, and duplicated into many copies. Paradoxically, the camera dealt with change and progression after it had already occurred. Opening the lens, fixing place and time, clicking the shutter, gave a mechanical one-time answer to a continuous question.

This intoxicating power of the camera lured a good many Montanans — who were already acutely aware of how rapidly the frontier had changed — into a historical frame of mind. A story needed to be told, an experience authenticated, and George Eastman's Kodak — smaller, cheaper, and easier to handle — helped them tell it. Feeling themselves and their land exceptional, Montanans — army officers, homesteaders, railroad engineers — attempted to show themselves and others the way they were and what they had done.

Not only Westerners but Americans generally on both sides of 1900 thought their world to be a vanishing one. Progress had brought sweeping nostalgia as well as bewildering innovation. Anxious conservationists such as Gifford Pinchot and John Muir saw America as a land of vanishing forests. Charles Russell and Zane Grey memorialized the eternally vanishing cowboy riding over the purple sage. Everything old was vanishing, including the Indian — that "vanishing American" who could now be commemorated on the Indian-head penny or opposite the extinct buffalo on the nickel. The perception was that Indians were what whites romantically and wistfully called "at the end of the trail."

Because the Blackfeet were perceived as one of the components of a vanishing frontier, whites attempted to reach back through time to document Blackfeet existence or at least recreate it. That was not easy. The Blackfeet had done little to chronicle the creation of their reservation life. Their oral traditions continued to reflect an earlier period of buffalo and war, confirming the old patterns, spurning the new. Picture-writing on tepees, shirts, and skins kept the stick-warrior exploits of the past in front of young and old. The reservation institutions, however, were not explored. The agent, the boarding school, the church, the trading post, all essentially imposed by whites, found their articulated reality only on sheets of paper.

Documents, written in English by whites, met the bureaucratic needs of government agencies. Institutional principle dictated that if money was spent, records had to be kept. Annual, semiannual, and quarterly reports had to be written. Financial audits had to be initiated, conducted, duplicated, analyzed. Inspection tours became routine.

This is the documentation that described the creation of the reservation and its visceral workings — there were treaties, real estate transactions, allotments, water rights, disbursement of funds, irrigation files. Yet in all of this scribbling, the daily life of individual families remained a blur. The customary acts that punctuated routine sometimes found expression, but only as single, significant markers that did not reveal much. So buying beef became a contract, marriage to Owl Woman a license, returning from the army across the sea a discharge. These agency documents, in their brisk, abbreviated fashion, traced the government's dealings with its "children" in a manner as skeletal as the simplified stick figures of horses and men rendered in earlier Piegan picture-writing.

The camera, however, allowed for a layered reality, for nuance and detail. A few photographs of the Blackfeet began to appear in the early 1880s, usually the work of army officers, government officials, and a few local white men associated with the agency. A. B. Coe, for example, came West to Fort Benton to teach school. Once there he married Isabel Cobell, the mixed-blood daughter of Joe and Mary Cobell, and moved to Old Agency where Mrs. Coe interpreted for the agency and Coe served as Superintendent of the agency school. While there he photographed individual Blackfeet (1890s) and wrote a column for a Cleveland, Ohio, newspaper.

Charles S. Francis was an early tourist who took pictures. Along with a small party of affluent sportsmen from New York, in 1888 Francis rode the St. Paul, Minneapolis, and Manitoba Railroad west through Dakota Territory to Great Falls, Montana, on his way to the mountains and streams of what would become Glacier National Park. Their "toggery weapons" included Marlin 45 caliber rifles, revolvers "with eight-inch barrels and forty-five bore," "fly and bait rods, trolling lines and spoons," and cameras. One cameraman used only dry plates and an other an Eastman film holder that used roll film, allowing for "forty-eight different exposures." With Joe Kipp as their guide, the sportsmen recorded their experiences as they hunted and fished; these included rare photographs of Old Agency, Kipp's store, and individual Blackfeet such as Cut Bank John. Camera activity was a form of verification. Government officials, schoolteachers, and tourists substantiated on negatives and paper prints their experiences and their reports.

The Blackfeet did not care who took their pictures in that period before the Willow Creek agency. After 1895, however, they did. George Bird Grinnell, Walter McClintock, and E. S. Curtis entered Blackfeet country with a professional approach to photography. Concerned as ethnographers as well as photographers, they were men with a mission who worked hard at understanding what they saw. Mad Wolf, chief and owner of the Beaver medicine bundle, purposely adopted McClintock so that he and his camera could dispel misunderstandings and misrepresentations. Mad Wolf wanted, McClintock wrote, "a white representative, who had lived sufficiently long among his people, to become familiar with their customs, religion, and manner of life, and would tell the truth about them to the white race." McClintock detailed that truth with his camera, and so did others even when they had no assignment.

Together McClintock and Curtis selected a nomadic past to photograph, one that by 1905–10 had almost slipped away. Photographing in what Susan Sontag has called "a mournful vision of loss," they preserved old artifacts, scenic landscapes, romantic camp scenes, and religious celebrations. They also painted, in black and white, two-dimensional pictures, reconstructions of a world that already had disappeared. Both men consciously ignored the tremendous changes that had transpired on the reservation since the collapse of the buffalo economy in 1884. Indian schools, the agency, the ration house, the log houses, and the attempts at raising hay, at cultivating vegetable gardens, at working on irrigation ditches do not appear in their photographs. Instead of catching life as it was being lived, these photographers — partly ethnographers, partly linguists, certainly social scientists — opted for a manner of life that was now vestigial. They were determined to record, in static fashion, the traditional culture as it had been employed to give authority to habits, rhythms, and patterns.

The McClintock-Curtis approach was highly selective. It also was deceptive, and consciously so. It focused on documenting sequential stages in religious ceremonies, on paraphernalia of parades, and on cataloging painted lodges. Sham warfare also drew their interest, as did older veterans of the intertribal war period who had the requisite degree of character etched into their pagan faces. McClintock and Curtis avoided modern intrusions. Not interested in an Indian present nor an Indian future, they reflected the romantic anxiety of their times — the desire to snatch away just in the nick of time an imperiled past that somehow because it was older was more real and better.

Other photographers with a very different purpose — making money — took surprisingly similar photographs. N. F. Forsyth of Butte, Montana, and J. H. Sherburne, the licensed trader in Browning, as well as Thomas B. Magee of Browning, tried to profit by selling popular "Indian views." Stereopticon slides, studio cards, post cards, tinted wall photographs, all emphasized a noble, savage, exotic Indian. Isolating colorful activities that met a ready demand, the diminished warriors now became paper heroes — more understandable and manageable. What Americans wanted to believe about the frontier, they could; what they wanted to forget was screened out, shoved beyond the defined edge of the purchased studio card or print.

The resulting photographs, both Curtis's heroic "The Three Chiefs," astraddle their fine horses, or Thomas B. Magee's popular stereopticon series marketed under Forsyth's name, belied the dismal reality of reservation life. However sincere, these attempts to advocate a past also carried with them the nagging suspicion that if Indians did not look like Indians, they weren't real. Moreover, they also failed to present the dizzy blur of disconnected, clashing images that disjointed reservation life. There was alienation in every house; the older Blackfeet culture could not be used to confirm, maintain, and reinforce the present. Curtis and McClintock knew this; so too did Thomas Magee and J. H. Sherburne. As proponents of a vanishing archaic, romantic, and marketable world, they suppressed any visible manifestation of these new uncertainties. The depressing conditions of reservation life interested no one. White society and white photographers wanted a sanitized Indian past before deterioration had set in so as to confirm their conviction that they could by prodigious effort salvage the vanishing American. If they could do that, they could also salvage their own vanishing America.

Other photographers with other purposes, however, emphasized specific changes — the progress that the Blackfeet were making in adapting to white ways. They were government officials in the Indian Service, missionaries, or school teachers who were professionally involved in the assimilation of the Blackfeet. They enjoyed photographing Blackfeet schoolchildren learning to sit at desks and playing musical instruments, just as they purposefully took pictures of Indians farming, making trips to Washington, D.C., and playing football. These prints demonstrated to doubters, white and Indian alike, that the Blackfeet actually were progressing into the self-sufficient, independent future envisioned.

After 1910, the largest group of photographers concerned with the Blackfeet consisted of popular "snapshooters." Local whites and tourists visiting the reservation and nearby Glacier Park carried their cameras to Sun Dance celebrations in Browning, or they turned them on reservation personalities and agency families. They too believed they were witnessing and preserving something special, different, and historical. They just knew this was the earlier frontier acting itself out a second time and, although they were too late the first time, now they were there.

Using simple cameras and operating them without much training, these occasional photographers did not secure perfect images. Normally they traded off clarity and composition. What they got in return were interesting, surprising pictures that no one else wanted. No romantic, soft-focused, engagement, but raw reality and a very different story. Aiming and clicking, they took pictures of cow camps, picnics, Fourth of July races, straight-eight Buicks, and kids. If they saw Blackfeet painting tepees with a Sears and Roebuck brush — great. They were not professional and you can see it. Their interests were random and momentary, yet they were ripe with detail and they recorded a world that the professionals disregarded as uninteresting and unworthy.

These tourists did not wish to compose a starchy, formal portrait in which the light had been squeezed from the subject's eyes. Nor did they wish to sell a product. They took as tourists the world as they found it — raw, without composure, and with no obvious meaning. Sometimes they were not even sure of *what* they had included in their snapshots. They blinked in dismay when their prints came back with trees emerging from heads, feet cut off, foreheads blurred. Sometimes the pictures returned with objects, connections, even people that had not been there, or rather had not been seen by the photographer. Yet these shortcomings should not concern us, for in the end they brought home to albums and drawing room boxes pieces of a tribal history.

After the turn of the century, the Great Northern Railway promoted tourism to its new facilities inside and adjacent to Glacier National Park. Referring to Glacier National Park as the "Switzerland of America," the railroad constructed imposing, rustic log lodges at Many Glacier, East Glacier Park, and Two Medicine Lake, and then joined these aristocratic accommodations with a road system that spiraled away from the rail line. Using the alpine theme, the Great Northern also built Swiss chalets on Cut Bank Creek, hired Swiss and Austrian climbing guides, and, in the European tradition, erected bells on mountain passes.

An even more popular Great Northern theme, used to attract tourists in the 1920s and 1930s, was to intertwine Glacier Park and the Blackfeet. Locating the Blackfeet, heroic and romantic, in the unspoiled majesty of Glacier Park carried immense appeal. Hiring such photographers as T. J. Hileman of Kalispell, the Great Northern placed the plains people, the Blackfeet, inside the park against a mountain backdrop. The combination was pure promotional gimmick and romantic nonsense. Tourists loved it.

Once established as an integral part of Glacier National Park, groups of Blackfeet people were hired by the Great Northern to promote rail travel to the West. Sent east, members of these groups danced in major cities, erected their tepees, and greeted visitors in their impressive native costumes. The Great Northern Railway also became the patron of the German-born artist Winold Reiss and commissioned him to paint Blackfeet portraits. In 1919, six years after arriving in America, Reiss began painting the Blackfeet in an arrangement that was beneficial to both. Year after year he painted literally hundreds of realistic, decorative portraits that enjoyed unprecedented popularity. Those bright images later came to grace attractive calendars, published and distributed annually since 1928 by the Great Northern. These calendars, featuring such Blackfeet as Lazy Boy, Bull Child, and Wades-in-Water, were designed to increase tourism to Glacier National Park by luring passengers west in the hope that they too could see and admire these "raiders of the plains" as well as the western scenery. Hotels, restaurants, and train stations also featured the Blackfeet in captivating poses by Reiss and others. The advertising prize, however, remained the calendar series. One year the company's calendar highlighted Rocky, the Great Northern goat, the next it featured Reiss's Blackfeet portraits.

The promotional campaign brought in customers. Eastern tourists streamed out West following the call of primitive adventure. Filing off the Great Northern trains whose lounges and literature had held out the vision of the Blackfeet in Glacier National Park, they discovered on the broad lawns in front of the East Glacier Lodge a real tepee encampment and Indians, decked out in their best finery and chanting a welcome. A number of full blood families "went up the park" where they were employed to camp, dance, demonstrate sign language, and "be colorful." Old warriors like Calf Tail often did a brisk business selling photographs of themselves which they then autographed with a pictograph. George Bull Child painted pictographic war stories of an earlier time on buckskin while Medicine Boss Ribs interested other tourists with his miniature tepees. Tourists had to bring back proof of this wondrous place to Philadelphia or Chicago; they did so by means of photographs, theirs or post cards, and calendars marketed by the railroad. The Blackfeet were too picturesque to be left behind without memento.

The real reservation world of the Blackfeet was removed from the tourists' photographs in place and psychology. Divorced from the promotional world of the Great Northern, the reservation Blackfeet struggled to survive the 1920s in poverty and obscurity.

No outsider appears consciously to have photographed the Blackfeet in this period — certainly not in any systematic fashion. Once in a while a tourist would slip down from "the Park" to look at Browning or maybe an inspector from Washington, D.C., would visit the full-blood communities of Starr School or Heart Butte, but little resulted. Agent Fred Campbell initiated a photographic survey of housing conditions upon assuming office in 1921, but his purpose was narrow. He wanted to show progress, but first he needed to document a base against which he could measure improvement. School teachers took pictures, too, but mainly what you would expect — classes assembled on the school steps, a few proud parents standing beside a graduate, or a couple of cute kids leering at the camera and making faces. The outsiders were gone or uninterested; it amounted to the same thing. After 1920 it was up to the Blackfeet themselves to take their own pictures.

Blackfeet Indians taking their own photographs was new. Indian men and women had learned to use other machines — sewing machines, wringer washers, Fresno-scrapers, steam tractors, and automobiles — but no one except George Henkel, a mixed blood who settled in the St. Mary-Babb area, used the camera. Photographing the Blackfeet had been a white endeavor. Whatever the photographs told of Blackfeet life, they represented the perspective of an outside observer and not that of a tribal participant.

Thomas B. Magee, although white, may have been an exception. He was a long-time resident of the reservation and understood the Blackfeet more than most. A sidekick of Joe Kipp and the first postmaster of Robare, he photographed out of interest as much as for money. His wife was Piegan, he was social, and the combination opened up many situations which he then photographed. His most productive years were from 1895 to 1915. By 1920 he had opened a photographic studio at Glacier National Park and lived just a short way out of East Glacier Park. When he died in July of 1930 he was the county clerk for Glacier County, living in Cut Bank, Montana. Unfortunately, most of his collection of negatives, files, prints, and effects was lost when his house in East Glacier burned to the ground in 1933.

After 1915 Thomas B. Magee and J. H. Sherburne gave up their serious efforts at photographing the Blackfeet. Their productive periods had been short and when the prospect of copyrighting views and selling post cards of the locals did not materialize, they turned to something else — business in Sherburne's case, politics in Magee's. Only George Henkel continued his impulse to document. It was very easy to abandon photographing the Blackfeet after 1915. Homesteaders filled up the spaces beyond the reservation boundaries. World War I became a national preoccupation, and after 1918 there was drought, influenza, and economic collapse. The reservation suffered from all of these. No one wanted to photograph failure, and between 1917 and 1940 there seemed to be little else.

So it was left to the Blackfeet themselves to document their own presence. That they did so, in however abbreviated a form, attests more to the fact that the Vielles, the Arrow Tops, the Tatseys — all reservation people — were stirred to capture their present. Let some one else have the past.

*Tourist photographer at the Sun Dance, ca. 1910*

Photographing the "old time" Sun Dances became a common practice for tourists. Glacier National Park attracted many after its opening in 1910, and after 1914 touring buses of the Great Northern Railway transported tourists to Browning. *Photo by J. H. Sherburne; courtesy of Sherburne Collection, UM Archives*

## Fish Wolf Robe at 1911 Sun Dance

Fish Wolf Robe, with Shrine pennant from Atlanta, Georgia, poses with his wife, Mary, and daughter. Such pennants, political buttons, and pins were welcomed adornment. Usually they were gifts from appreciative tourists, and they came to mark dress changes as the Sun Dance, in addition to being a religious celebration, became a tourist "show." *Photo courtesy of Sherburne Collection, UM Archives*

## *"Blackfeet encampment in front of East Glacier Lodge, September"*

By the late 1920s tourism represented another method of survival for some. The Great Northern Railroad promoted travel to Glacier National Park and Blackfeet country. Using the promotional gimmick of placing the Plains people, the Blackfeet, in the majestic splendor of the park, which it served, the Great Northern hired certain Indian families to camp outside their lodges in East Glacier and Many Glacier and to greet wealthy tourists arriving by train from the East. *Photo courtesy of Fred Des Rosier*

## Three Bears at wheel of Glacier Park tour bus

Eastern dudes were still driven to Browning to see the spectacle of "real" Indians. Costumed chauffeurs only added to the excitement. The photographer called this group "Bear's family." *Photo by Walter Shelley Phillips; courtesy of University of Washington Library*

*Medicine Boss Ribs selling tepees to tourists
in front of East Glacier Lodge*

Twelve miles from Browning and the Blackfeet Agency, "up at the park," some of the traditional Blackfeet would dance for the tourists or sell trinkets and pose for pictures.
*Photo courtesy of MSU Special Collections*

*Calf Tail post card with signature, 1929*

It was not unusual to find old-time warriors "up at the park" selling photographs of themselves to tourists without cameras and then autographing them with pictographs. Although demeaning, appealing to the tourists kept individual Blackfeet and their families fed and clothed in an era of poverty. *Photo courtesy of Mae Vallance*

*Off to Hollywood to make a movie — Browning Station, 1939*

Left to right: Turtle, Little Blaze, unidentified, Arrow Top Knot, unidentified, Albert Mad Plume, unidentified, Tom Many Guns, Mike Bad Old Man, Victor Chief Coward

*Suzanne and the Mounties,* starring Shirley Temple and Randolph Scott, featured Martin Pepion of Browning in a prominent role. By 1939 Indians all over the West were being rediscovered following years of abandonment and neglect. Yet while full bloods were still very visible working the tourists of Glacier National Park, or on this occasion making a movie in Hollywood, their numbers dwindled. Surviving by their wits, they continued being what they had always been, Blackfeet. *Photo courtesy of MSU Special Collections*

*Jack Big Moon, unidentified, John Ground, and Irving Little
Plume(?) in the majestic grandeur of Glacier National Park*

*Photo courtesy of Glacier National Park Archives*

# Epilogue

Althoug some cultures die hard, slow deaths, others survive long after most people have given them up for dead. The Blackfeet culture, however diminished, continued in the shape of values, in the daily motions that dictate perspective, and in cultural nostalgia.

After World War II the Blackfeet, as well as everyone else in America, adjusted to changes that had come with the war effort and that now could not be stopped. This did not mean ceasing to be Indian or to identify with tribal interests, but it did mean moving away from earlier circumstances, from earlier values. Left behind were traditional "long hair" parents, isolated reservation communities such as Starr School or Heart Butte, Babb or Two Medicine, and ranch work or no work. That migration away to Browning, to more excitement, to a different kind of work with the agency, town, or county crews, to better pay, led to other outward journeys. Young people wanted a better car, better command of writing skills, a nice house with trips to Great Falls. They wanted to move away and become, as one phrased it, "another kind of Indian."

As soon as those young people developed the skills and the confidence to move on, many of the more talented and adventuresome did. They fled to Great Falls, to Seattle, Spokane, or Portland, where they thought a better life awaited them as machinists, greengrocers working for Buttrey's, Boeing welders, or students enrolled in college.

The number of Piegan-speaking elders contracted to a dangerous level. Most Blackfeet after 1940 no longer spoke the language of their fathers, although a considerable number understood a bit when spoken to. It was a passive language, however, and not muscular and active. Blackfeet culture without the cement of language, distinct and defining, slowly crumbled away like a sandy bank.

The cultural base experienced further erosion through continued intermarriage and a willingness to settle for less. Many individuals did not understand the corrosive influence of moving toward a "better life." The phrase carried with it an unspoken assumption that white culture was more progressive and advanced than their own. To believe this was to make it so, and too many came to view their past as something to be overcome. The Blackfeet were not unique in this belief, but it did lead to a greater split between old and new on the reservation than elsewhere.

The majority of the Blackfeet after the war simply found their culture undemanding. There were reservation dances, basketball games, and shopping sprees to Great Falls, interwoven with a "giveaway," an occasional "medicine smoke," or grandchildren being given Indian names. "Indian Days" replaced the midsummer Sun Dance — setting up the tepee, now canvas, at the edge of Browning in the traditional place, still happened as did camping out with woodstove and grandma, dancing until early morning, and watching isolated pockets of religious prayer among the elders.

The traditional and the new Indian worlds fused gradually with the pressing white one. A style of life emerged that was predictable, routine, and definitely reservation. It was also less clearly Blackfeet. This bland mixture reflected not only what Indian people wanted, but what was possible. The majority of the Blackfeet, whatever their "mix," wanted more than their parents had had, wanted more choice. As young couples imagined their possible futures, the cherished past disintegrated into disconnected practices, convictions, and beliefs. Experience too white and too modern compromised each and everyone.

The older people talked. They bragged a little about their children, fed their memories with talk while sitting in the afternoon sun in front of the Mint Saloon in Browning, or resting with their backs against the log wall of the Round Hall in Heart Butte. The reservation allowed for that as it did for endless cups of coffee, woodsmoke, and kitchen tables. "Talking Indian" to one another, they retold stories. Their children and grandchildren listened, sometimes played awhile or wandered off, then picked up the talk later on; it was informal instruction — an unselfconscious learning of some of the tribal experiences with buffalo, hunting, and counting coup even though these children could not repeat them. Because that past was not repeatable, however, it was inevitable that the world of the fathers slipped away. This wearing away of the former world did not occur at an even rate. Some practices and values, like particles of rock, retained their grit longer, but in time the Blackfeet changed. Gradually young adults on the reservation entered American life on more and more favorable terms. Children spent more years in glass and brick schools and parents led easier lives filled with freezers, antibiotics, and snowmobiles. In this process keeping score was difficult. There was immeasurable loss and gain. Yet the Blackfeet still retained a tribal past that resonated.

Questions would remain for the post-war years of the 1950s and 1960s as the Blackfeet more completely entered into the mainstream of American life while remaining in their circle of tradition. Identity, however, would not be the focus, renewal and revival would. Blackfeet men and women, mixed bloods or not, recognized that no, they were not the same as their mothers and fathers, nor need they be. They had not lived out their lives in the same way, but they were still Blackfeet, however many cultural and social boundaries may have been crossed, however much time had passed.

# Select Bibliography

T HIS IS a short guide to further reading as well as an indication of the literature upon which the text is based. These are general studies (for the most part) covering areas of wider historical interest and are authoritative in their treatment.

Blackman, Margaret. "Posing the American Indian." *Natural History* 89 (October 1980), 69–74.

Comes At Night, George. *Roaming Days: Warrior Stories.* Browning, MT: Blackfeet Heritage Program, 1978.

Dempsey, Hugh A. "The Amazing Death of Calf Shirt." *Montana: The Magazine of Western History* 3 (1953), 65–72.

———. *A Blackfoot Winter Count.* Calgary: Glenbow Alberta Institute, Occasional Paper 1, 1965.

———. *Crowfoot, Chief of the Blackfeet.* Norman: University of Oklahoma Press, 1972.

———. *Charcoal's World.* Lincoln: University of Nebraska Press, 1979.

Ege, Robert J. *Tell Baker to Strike Them Hard: Incident on the Marias, 23 January 1870.* Fort Collins, CO: Old Army Press, 1970.

Ewers, John C. *The Story of the Blackfeet.* Indian Life and Customs Pamphlets, no. 6, 1944.

———. *Blackfeet Crafts.* Indian Handcraft Pamphlets, no. 9, 1945.

———. *The Horse in Blackfoot Indian Culture.* U.S. Bureau of American Ethnology, Bulletin 159, 1955.

———. *The Blackfeet: Raiders on the Northwestern Plains.* Norman: University of Oklahoma Press, 1958.

———. "When Red and White Met." *Western History Quarterly* 2 (April 1971), 133–50.

———. "The Influence of the Fur Trade upon the Indians of the Northern Plains." Pp. 6–7 in Malvina Bolus, ed., *People and Pelts.* Winnipeg, 1972.

———. "A Century and a Half of Blackfeet Picture-Writing." *American Indian Art* (Summer 1983), 52–61.

"Five-Year Program on the Blackfeet Indian Reservation." *The Indian Leader* 26 (1923).

Foley, Michael F. *An Historical Analysis of the Administration of the Blackfeet Indian Reservation by the United States, 1855–1950's.* Indian Claims Commission, Docket Number 279-D, n.d.

Gold, Douglas. *A Schoolmaster with the Blackfeet Indians.* Caldwell, ID: Caxton Printers, 1963.

Ground, Mary. *Grass Woman Stories.* Browning, MT: Blackfeet Heritage Program, 1978.

Grinnell, George Bird. *Blackfoot Lodge Tales.* New York, 1892.

———. *The Story of the Indian.* New York, 1895.

———. "The Lodges of the Blackfeet." *American Anthropologist* 3 (1901), 650–68.

———. *Blackfeet Indian Stories.* New York, 1913.

Harrod, Howard C. *Mission Among the Blackfeet.* Norman: University of Oklahoma Press, 1971.

Holterman, Jack. "Seven Blackfeet Stories." *Indian Historian* 3 (1970), 39–43.

Lancaster, Richard. *Piegan: A Look from Within at the Life, Times, and Legacy of the American Indian Tribe.* Garden City, NY: Doubleday, 1966.

Lewis, Oscar. *The Effects of White Contact upon Blackfoot Culture.* Monographs of the American Ethnological Society, no. 6. 1942.

Linderman, Frank B. *Blackfeet Indians.* St. Paul: Great Northern Railway, 1935. (Pictures by Winold Reiss.)

Many Guns, Tom. *Pinto Horse Rider.* Browning, MT: Blackfeet Heritage Program, 1979.

McClintock, Walter. *Old North Trail.* London: Macmillan, 1910.

————. *Old Indian Trails.* Boston: Houghton Mifflin, 1923.

————. "The Tragedy of the Blackfoot." *Southwest Museum Papers* 3 (1930), 1–53.

McFee, Malcolm. *Modern Blackfeet: Montanans on a Reservation.* New York: Holt, Rinehart and Winston, 1972.

Parsons, Jackie. *The Educational Movement of the Blackfeet Indians, 1840–1979.* Browning, MT: Blackfeet Heritage Program, 1980.

Schoenberg, Wilfred. "Historic St. Peter's Mission: Landmark of the Jesuits and the Ursulines among the Blackfeet." *Montana: The Magazine of Western History* 11 (1961), 68–85.

Schultz, James Willard. *My Life as an Indian.* New York: Macmillan, 1907.

————. *Friends of My Life as an Indian.* Boston: Houghton Mifflin, 1923.

————. *Blackfeet and Buffalo: Memories of Life among the Indians.* Norman: University of Oklahoma Press, 1962.

Sharp, Paul. "Blackfeet of the Border: One People Divided." *Montana: The Magazine of Western History* 20 (1970), 2–15.

————. *Whoop-Up Country.* Norman: University of Oklahoma Press, 1978.

Steward, J. H. *The Blackfoot.* Berkeley, CA, 1934.

Wessel, Thomas R. *Historical Report on the Blackfeet Reservation on Northern Montana.* Indian Claims Commission, Docket No. 279-D, 1975.

————. "Agriculture on the Reservation: The Case of the Blackfeet, 1885–1935." *Journal of the West* 18 (October 1979), 17–24.

West, Helen B. "Starvation Winter of the Blackfeet." *Montana: The Magazine of Western History* 10 (1959), 34–44.

————. "Blackfoot Country." *Montana: The Magazine of Western History* 10 (1960), 34–44.

Wissler, Clark. *Material Culture of the Blackfoot Indians* and *The Sun Dance of the Blackfoot Indians.* American Museum of Natural History, Anthropological Papers 16 (1918), 223–70.

Woehlke, Walter V. "Hope for the Blackfeet." *Sunset Magazine* (December 1923).


For further bibliographical information pertaining to the Blackfeet of Montana, see:


Hill, Edward E. *Guide to Records in the National Archives of the United States Relating to American Indians.* Washington, D.C.: National Archives and Records Service, General Services Administration, 1981.

Dockstadter, Frederick J. *The American Indian in Graduate Studies: A Bibliography of Theses and Dissertations.* 2d ed. New York: Museum of the American Indian, Heye Foundation, 1973.

Prucha, Francis P. *A Bibliographical Guide to the History of Indian-White Relations in the United States.* Chicago: University of Chicago Press, 1977.

# Index

Agents. *See* Indian agents; Old Agency; Willow Creek Agency
Allen, Edgar A., 97
All Over, Chief, *182*
All Over family, 182
All Over, George, *182*
American Fur Company, 26, 27
Anthropologists and ethnographers, 141, 189
Arrow Top Knot, *186, 201*
Arrow Tops, the, 193
Assiniboine, 10, 93
Aubrey, Tom, *105*
Augare, Agnes Guardipee, *158*

Babb, 49, 203
Badger Creek, 169. *See also* Old Agency
Bad Marriage, *185*
Bad Marriage, James, *62*
Bad Old Man, Mike, *186, 201*
Baker, Eugene, 27
Baker Massacre, 7, 21, 27
Barker, photo by, 103
Basket making, *131*
Beacom, John, 17; photos by, 17, 21
Bear Chief (the younger), *37, 64, 65,* 71
Bear Child (Lewis Plenty Treaties), *121*
Bear Child, Josephine, *53*
Bear Medicine, John, *183*
Beaver trade, 4
Big Beaver, Rosy, *134*
Big Brave's Son, *152*
Big Moon, Jack, *i, xii, 92, 201*
Big Nose, Mrs., *77*

Birch Creek, 170
Bird, John, *30*
Bird Rattler, *125, 185*
Bird, Sam, *105*
Bite, Mrs. Harry, *150*
Black Bull, *89*
Blackfeet Indian Reservation: location of, 3–4; boundary changes, 7, 10, 12, 13, 37; boundary controlled, 48, 98
Blackfeet population, 7, 8, 98, 101, 138
Blackfeet tribes, 4–8
"Blackfoot Nation," 5
Black Horse society, *93*
Black-Patched-Moccasin Band, 33
Black Weasel, *65, 186*
Bloods, 4, 5, 6, 7, 95
Boarding schools. *See* Schools
Boss Ribs, Barney, 149
Boss Ribs, Dennis, 149
Boss Ribs, Emily, 149
Boss Ribs, Joe, 56
Boss Ribs, Medicine, *185,* 192, *198*
Bostwick children, *159*
Bostwick, Frank, 159
Bostwick, Mary, 159
Brave Dogs, 88
Bremner, Flora, *184*
Bremner, Ida, 167
Broadwater, W. C., 42, 101
Brocky (Tail Feathers Coming Over the Hill), *37, 63*
Brown, Diamond R., 41
Brown, Joe, *65*
Browning, 38, *41,* 49, 97, 100, 126, 127, 144, 169, 170, *186,* 192, *201,* 204; Browning

High School, xiii, 117; first mayor, *105;* moonlight school, *130;* Southsiders, 46; tennis court, *51*
Browning, Daniel, 41
Buck, Charles, 65
Buffalo Body, *120*
Buffalo Dung band, x
Buffalo hide trade, 4–5, 8
Buffalo Hide, Willie, 150
Buffalo horns, *140*
Bull Calf, *65*
Bull Child, *77, 87,* 191
Bull Child, George, 192
Bull Shoe, Joe, *120*
Burd, Levi, 65, *125*
Burial grounds, *36*
Burial scaffold, *xx*

Calf Looking, Mrs., *134*
Calf Robe, Joe, *162*
Calf Robe, Sam, *133*
Calf Shirt, *95*
Calf Tail, *96,* 191, *199*
Campbell, Fred C., 101–2, 110, 111, 112, 113, 114, 115, 117, 119, *120,* 123, 125, 192
Camp crier (herald), *74, 146*
Canadian government, 7
Carlisle Indian School, 39
Carroll, J. B., S.J., 67–68
Catlin, John, 98
Cattle raising, 7, 8, 9, 11, 35, 97–100, 102, *103,* 104, 105, 119; dipping vats, *107;* fence around reservation, 98; slaughterhouse, *15, 52*
Chandler, Devon, xxi
Chase, E. L.: photos by, 50, 51, 59, 65

Chewing Black Bones, *177*
Choate, Frank, *172*
Choate, J. N., 37
Choteau, Pierre, 26; Pierre Choteau Company, 28
Chouquette, Charles, *26, 28, 29*
Chouquette, Henry, *30*
Chouquette, Rosa Lee, 26, 29
Civilian Conservation Corps/ Indian Agency, 126, 127
Clark, George, *53*
Clarke, Malcolm, *65*
Clements, Walter M., 12
Coat, Broken Leg, *156*
Coat, Ida Oscar, *156*
Coat, The, *156*
Cobell, Isabel. *See* Coe, Mrs. A. B.
Cobell, Joe, 29, 188
Cobell, Mary, 188
Coe, A. B., 21, 188; photos by, 18, 19
Coe, Mrs. A. B. (Isabel Cobell), 29, 188
Connelly, B., *53*
Conrad, William G., 98
Cooke, Lorenzo W., 11–12
Council, Tribal. *See* Tribal Council
Coup sticks, 86; counting coup, 81, 169
Coward, Victor Chief, *201*
Cowboys, *103, 124*
Craft clubs, *134, 136*
Crazy Dogs. *See* Mad Dogs
Crofts family, 26
Croft, Mrs., *31*
Crow, Chief, *65*
Crow Indians, 26, 49; medicine bundle, *183;* tepee, *49*
Cumming, Alfred, 5
Curly Bear, *64, 65, 155*
Curtis, E. S., 189–90
Cut Bank, 48
Cut Bank Creek, 102
Cut Bank Creek boarding school, 39, *54, 59*
Cut Bank John, 188
Cypress Hills Massacre, 104

Damiani, Father, 24
Dance hall, *152*
Dawson, Tom, *28*

Department of the Interior, 122
De Roche, Annie, *167*
De Roche, Benjamin, *167*
De Roche, Charley, *167*
De Roche, Julia Wolftail, *167*
De Smet, Father Pierre-Jean (Long Teeth), *31*
Devereaux, Elijah Jeff, *104,* 105
Devereaux, Henry, *105*
Devereaux, Spyna, *104*
Dipping vats, *107*
Dog Gun, Tom, *133*
Double Runner, Eddie, *186*
Doves, *88, 169*
Drums, *89, 94*
Dusty Bull, Minnie, *111*

Eastman, George, 187
Edkins, Helen, 28
Edwards, Ella, *184*
Edwards, George, *44*
Elk, Chief, *87*
Elk Horn, *74, 146, 152*
Elk Horn, son of, *146*
Elliott Studio, photo by, 130
Enlarged Homestead Act (1909), 49
Evans, Aloysius, *133*
Evans, Victor J., *125*
Ewers, John, xv, 100

Farming, 97–102, 109, 110, 111, 112, 113; drought, 101, 114; gopher bounty, *114;* hay crop, *116;* Midwinter Fair, *117, 118;* wheat harvesting, *115*
Fat Melters (Grease Melters), 66, 74, 146
*Field and Stream,* 12
Firewood hauling, *165*
Fish Wolf Robe, *88, 185, 195*
Fish Wolf Robe, daughter of, *195*
Fish Wolf Robe, Mary, *195*
Five-Year Industrial Program (Piegan Farming and Livestock Association), 102, 111, 112, 119, 120, 121
Flintsmoker, Orcelia, *110*
Flintsmoker, Peter, *110*

Flintsmoker, Under Beaver, *110*
Flood of 1964, xiii
Floweree, Dan, 103
Floweree Cattle Company, 98
Forsyth, N. F., 189, 190; photo by, 157
Fort Benton, 5, 188; agency established at, 6–7
Fort Shaw, 6, 21, 27; school, 39, 62
Fort Union, 5
Four Horns, *37, 63, 64, 154*
"Four Persons" Agency, 13
Fourth of July, 66–67
Francis, Charles S., 188

"Ghost Ridge," 14
Gill, D. L.: photo by, 64
Glacier National Park, 12, 37, 171, 191, 192, 194, *196, 197, 198, 199,* 201, *202*
Gold, Douglas, 128
Gold seekers, 37
Good Gun, *18, 120, 186*
Gopher bounty, *114*
Gordon, Tim, 13
Goss, Lomie, *106*
Grant, Jimmy, *30*
Grant, Ulysses S., 7, 23
Grass burning, 173
Grass dance, *93,* 152
Grazing: illegal, 98, 103; permits, 98–99, 102
Grease Melters. *See* Fat Melters
Great Northern Railroad, x, 9–10, 11, 12, 98, 101, 140, 191, 192, 194, 196
Green Grass Bull, 45, *186*
Grey, Zane, 187
Grinnell, George Bird, 12, 97, *141,* 189
Gros Ventres, 5, 10
Ground, John, *111, 201*
Ground, Mary (Grass Woman), 25, 54
Guardipee, Florence, *184*
Guardipee, Old Lady, *158*

Hair Parters, 93
Hamilton, Robert, 111, 125, 170

Hannon, Olga Ross: photos by, 134, 172, 173, 176
Hard-Top-Knots, 66
Harrison, Frank, *168*
Harrison, Mrs. Frank (Pipe Woman), *168*
Hatch, Edwin A. C., 6
Hazlett, Stuart, 65
Headdresses, *73, 76, 92, 185*
Heart Butte, 102, 109, 112, 170, 192, 203; farmers, *120;* moonlight school, *128, 129, 133*
Heart Butte Round Hall, 129, 131, 204
Heavy Breast, Owen, *116*
Heavy Breast, Rosa, *116*
Heavy Runner, 7, 21, 27
Heavy Runner, Mrs., *176*
*Helena Herald,* 9
Henderson, Lizzie, 24
Henkel family, 26
Henkel, George, 192
Hileman, T. J., 191; photo by, xiv
Hill, James, 9
Holy Family Mission school, *24,* 39; band, *25*
Homesteading, 101, 109, 193
Horn, Tom, *18*
Horse-dancing, 79
Horse effigies, *72, 93*
Horse-pulling contest, *106*
Horse raiders, 34
Hudson's Bay Company, 4

Imoda, Father John, *23*
Indian agents, 10–12, 38–39; challenge to authority of chiefs, 63, 65; and economic development, 97–102; educational responsibilities of, 23. *See also* Old Agency; Willow Creek Agency
"Indian Days," 204
Indian Office. *See* United States government
*Indian Sentinel,* 67
Indian Service. *See* United States government
Interpreters, 29, 188
Irrigation projects, 97, 98, 99–100, *108*

Jamison, Laura Walters, *184*
Jenkins (Washington inspector), 53
Jesuits (Black Robes), 21, *23, 31;* banned from reservation, 23; commentary on Sun Dance, 67–68
Johnson-O'Malley Act, Committee, xv
Jones, W. A., 99
Juneau, Old Lady, *149*

Kainah (Bloods), 4. *See also* Bloods
Kennerly family, 26
Kipp, Billy, *65*
Kipp family, 26
Kipp, Joe (Raven Quiver), *27, 28,* 30, 41, 42, *63,* 188, 192; Kipp's water system, *45*
Kipp, Mrs., *31*
Kiser: photos by, 72, 73
Kit Foxes, 88

Lame Bear, *153*
Lame Bull, 5
Lame Bull's Treaty, 5, 6, 7
Lapwai, Idaho, 184
Law, system of, 46
Lazy Boy, *186,* 191
Lewis, Meriwether, 4
Little Badger Women's Club, *135*
Little Bear, *63*
Little Blaze, *181, 201*
Little Blaze, John, *131*
Little Blaze, Mrs. (Snakes-in-the-Grass), *181*
Little Dog, *33,* 37, *63, 64,* 65, 88
Little Otter Woman (Mrs. Running Crane), *158*
Little Owl, *152*
Little Plume, *37, 63*
Little Plume, Irving, *152, 201*
Logging crew, *32, 127*
Lone Walker, 26
Lucero, Dick, *166*

Mad Dogs, 33, *74, 78;* Crazy Dogs, *84, 90*
Mad Plume, Albert, *113, 119, 201*

Mad Plume, Fred, *113*
Mad Plume, Irene, *113*
Mad Plume, Susan, *113, 119*
Mad Wolf, *32, 111,* 189
Mad Wolf, Charlie, *111*
Mad Wolf, Mark, *111*
Mad Wolf, Rosie, *111*
Magee, Thomas, 189, 190, 192; photos by, xviii, xx, 20, 24, 25, 26, 35, 36, 41, 47, 78, 79, 82, 85, 90, 93, 95, 96, 146, 147, 148, 149, 151, 153, 154, 156, 158, 161, 162
Many Guns, Tom, xv, xvii, 56, *201*
Many Hides, *111*
Marceau, Alex, *123*
Marceau family, 123
Marceau, Maggie, *157*
Marceau, Pete, *157*
Marceau, Peter, Sr., *164*
*Masterkey,* xv
Matson, W. H., 53
McClintock, Walter, 72, 189, 190; photos by, ii, iv, x, xvi, 74, 81, 83, 84
McFatridge, Arthur E., *48,* 49, *91*
McFatridge, Mrs., *49*
Medicine Bull, *18*
Medicine Bull, Tom, *93*
Medicine bundles, *162, 183*
Medicine lodge, 66, *73, 76, 78, 80–82, 83, 84–87, 90–92, 94, 95–96,* 170, *174, 175, 176, 177*
Medicine men, *77, 78,* 80, *87,* 95
Medicine Owl, 71
Medicine Smoke ceremony, *183,* 204
Methodist Church, 23
Middle Rider, *185*
Miller, Zack, *64,* 65
Milwaukee Railroad, 101
Mining activity, 12, 37
Mint Saloon, *186,* 204
Mission schools. *See* Schools
Monroe, Angus, 29
Monroe family, 26
Monroe, Hugh (Rising Wolf), 26, 104

Monroe, Mrs. Hugh (Sino-pah), 26
Monroe, Old John, *26, 31*
Monroe, Mrs. John, *31*
Monteath, James, 98, 99
Moonlight schools, *128–33*
Mosquitoes, 88
Mountain Chief, *64, 65, 72, 185*
Mountain Chief, Mrs., *72*
Mountain Chief, John, *106, 186*
Movie making, 201
Mud Head, *172*
Muir, John, 187

Nequette, Louis, 26
Night Gun, John, *30*
No Coat, *46, 65, 120, 131, 147, 148*
No Coat, daughter of, *147*
No Coat, wife of, *148*
Northern Blackfeet, 4, 5, 6, 7
Northern Pacific, 101
Northern Pikuni (Northern Piegans), 4, 7
Northsiders, 44
North West Mounted Police, 7

Oil mining, 49, 102, *122*
Old Agency (Badger Creek), 8, 9–12, *13–37*, 63, 188; employees, *17*; schools, 21
Old Person, *35*
Old Person, Mrs., *35*
Old Person, Juniper, *111*
Old Person Number Two, *35*
"Old Ration Place," *13, 14*
Otter medicine bundle, *162*; Otter tepee, *72, 145, 149*
Owl Child, *64, 65*
Owl Woman, 188

Paul, Bea, *184*
"Peace Policy," 21, 23
Pepion, Louise, *134*
Pepion, Martin, 201
Percival place, *107*
Perrine, James, *65*
Phillips, Walter Shelley: photos by, 86, 155, 197

Photographic trends, 171, 187–93; post cards, *200*; tourist photographers, 191–92, *194, 197*
Piegan Farming and Livestock Association, 102, *111. See also* Five-Year Industrial Program
Piegans, 4, 5, 6, 7, 95; braves, *18*; chiefs, *37*, 63
Pigeons, 88
Pinchot, Gifford, 187
Pipe Woman, *168*
Plenty Treaties, Lewis (Bear Child), *121*
Police, Indian, 33, 34, 46, *47*, 48
Pollock, William C., 12
Population, Blackfeet, 7, 8, 98, 101, 138
Post, Helen M.: photo by, 137
Potts, Anna, *134*
Prando, Father Peter, 23, 24

Racine, Tiny, *134*
Railroads, 5, 101. *See also* Great Northern Railroad
Rainbow Lodge, *70*
Ranchers, white, 98–99
Rattlesnakes, 95
Red Head, Old, *129*
Reevis, Charles, *125, 152*
Reiss, Winold, 191
Reservation. *See* Blackfeet Indian Reservation
Rides-at-the-Door, *137, 186*
Rivois, Charles, 26, 28
Robare, 27, 48
Robinson, H. F.: photos by, 143, 145
Rodin, Baptiste, 26
Roundine, Sam, *53*
Running Crane, *37, 63, 65*, 158
Running Crane, Mrs. (Little Otter Woman), *158*
Running Crane, Judge, *46*
Running Crane, Old Man, *44*
Russell, Bill, *64*
Russell, Charles, 187

Saint Mary's Canal, *108*
Saint Mary's Lake, *142*
Saint Peter's Mission, 21, 23

Salway, Bob, *124*
Salway, Jason, *124*
Sanderville, Richard, *65, 120*
Schildt, Harry, *53*
Schmautz, Gary, ix
Schools, 39; Agency school at Badger Creek, *21*, 23; baking class, 55; Cut Bank Creek boarding school, 39, *54, 59*; Fort Shaw, 39, 62; mission schools, 21, *23, 24, 25*, 39; moonlight schools (for adults), *128–33*; sewing class, *54*; uniforms, 59; Victorian lady teacher, *22*; Willow Creek boarding school, 11, 39, 45, *53, 55, 56, 57*
Schultz, James Willard, 125
Scott, Randolph, 201
Sewing machine, *151*
Sham warfare, *79*, 189
Sharp (Piegan artist), x
Sheep raising, 102
Sherburne, J. H., 49, 100, 101, 189, 190, 192; photos by, 16, 34, 42, 53, 54, 55, 56, 70, 71, 75, 76, 91, 94, 144, 152, 194
Sherburne, J. L.: photos by, 52, 106, 108
Sherburne Mercantile, *42, 43, 44, 106, 141*
Shoot, Bill, *172*
Short Face, *111, 179*
Shortman, Mike, *90*
Siksika (Blackfoot), 4
Sinopah. *See* Monroe, Sinopah
Sioux, 10
Skunks, 66
Slaughterhouse, *15, 52*
Smallpox, 7, 8
Snakes-in-the-Grass, *181*
Sontag, Susan, 189
Southern Pikuni (Southern Piegans), 4, 6
Southsiders, 46
Spanish, Nora, *134*
Spearson, Martha, *110*
Split Ears, *65, 114, 152*
Spotted Bear, 109
Spotted Eagle, *xviii, 87*
Spotted Eagle, Good Victory, *132*
Spotted Eagle, Jim, *129*

Spotted Eagle, Tom, *129, 172*
Stabs-Down-By-Mistake, *88, 89, 137*
Starr School, 170, 192, 203
Starvation Winter of 1883–84, 8, 14, 23
Steell, George, 12, 40, 50, *63*
Stehakee, *111*
Stevens, Isaac I., 5, 27
Stone, Forrest, 102, 128
Strong, Melvin D., *120*
Sun Dance, 66–68, *69–96*, 170, *178*, 204; efforts to eliminate, 67; encampments, *151, 163, 164, 172, 176, 177, 194, 195;* moved to Fourth of July, 66. *See also* Medicine lodge; Vow woman
Sun Dance Lodge, 169
Sure Chief, *131*
*Suzanne and the Mounties,* 201
Sweat lodge, *78, 173*
Swims Under, *18*

Tail Feathers Coming Over the Hill (Brocky), *37, 63*
Takes Gun, Mike, *111*
Tanning hides, *145*
Tatsey family, 193
Tatsey, Joe, *64*
Temple, Shirley, 201
Tennis court, *51*
Tepees, *xiv, 69–72, 74, 75, 142, 180, 196, 197,* 204; "Bear Chief's War Lodge," *71;* Crow, *49;* for tourists, *199;* Otter, *72, 145, 149;* painting of, *181,* 190; "Rainbow Lodge," *70;* sewn canvas, 151; Snake, 71
Three Bears, *83, 197*
Three Calf, *177*
Three Sons, 10
Tourism, 191–92, *194–201;* post cards, *200;* tour bus, *198*
Traders, licensed, 27, 42, 43, 44, 101; stores, *30, 42, 43, 44. See also* Kipp, Joe; Sherburne Mercantile
Travois, 142, *144*

Treaties: council meetings, 27; Lame Bull's Treaty, 5–7; Treaty Commission, 10; Treaty Number Seven, 7; Treaty of 1887, 10, 11
Tribal Council, 39, *65, 137,* 170; against grazing, 98; and oil development, 122; delegation to Washington, D.C., *63, 64*
Tribes, 4–8
Tuberculosis sanitarium, 184
Turtle, *172, 179, 201*
Two Medicine, 134, 169, 203

Uhlenbeck, C. C., xv
United States government: agreement quoted, 38; census (1880), 8; delegations of Piegans to Washington, D.C., *63, 64;* Indian Office, 97, 99, 101, 107, 110; Indian policy, 39; Indian Service, 38, 66, 98, 99, 101, 102, 110; "land allotment," 49; payments from, 10, 11, 12, 37, 38; relief programs, *126, 127;* and Sun Dance, 66. *See also* Indian agents; Treaties
U.S. Indian Claims Commission, 98
U.S. Reclamation Service, 108
Upham family, 26
Upham, Mrs., *31*
Ursuline sisters, 24

Vallance, Mae, 131; photos by, 132, 135
Vielle family, 193
Vielle, Mrs., 150, 181
Vow woman, 66, *76,* 78, 170, 173, *176*

Wades-in-Water, 46, *148, 152,* 191
Wades-in-Water, wife of, *148*

Walters, Alice, *184*
War Bonnet, *152*
Warrior societies, 88
Water for farming, 98. *See also* Irrigation projects
Water projects (relief programs), 126
Water system, *45*
Weather booth, *87, 177*
Weather dancing, *87,* 170
Wessel, Thomas, 98
Wheat harvesting, *115*
Whiskey Gap, 48
Whiskey trade, 6, 7, 8, 27
White Calf, 7, 10, *19,* 24, *37, 63, 64, 137*
White Calf, Jim, *186*
White Calf, Two Guns, *125*
White Grass, *x, 37, 63*
White Grass, Paul, *111*
White influence on the reservation, 26, 39, 138–39, *140–68,* 190, 203–4
White Quiver, *34, 92, 120, 125*
White Swan, Charles, *166*
Williams, Susie, 29
Williamson, Mae, *134*
Willits and Scriver, 42
Willow Creek Agency, 12, 38–39, *40,* 41, 42, 43, 44, 45, 46, *50,* 52
Willow Creek boarding school, 11, 39, 45, *53, 55, 56, 57*
Winter count, ix
Wolf Plume, *65*
Wolf Plume, Mrs. (Strikes First), *132, 176*
Women: clothing traditions of, *161;* clubs, *134, 135;* in headdresses, *73;* in Sun Dance parade, *178;* three generations, *158. See also* Vow woman
World War II, 170–71
Worm People, 66
Wren, Malenda, *29*

Yellow Kidney, *18*
Young, John W., 8, 13, 23, 33

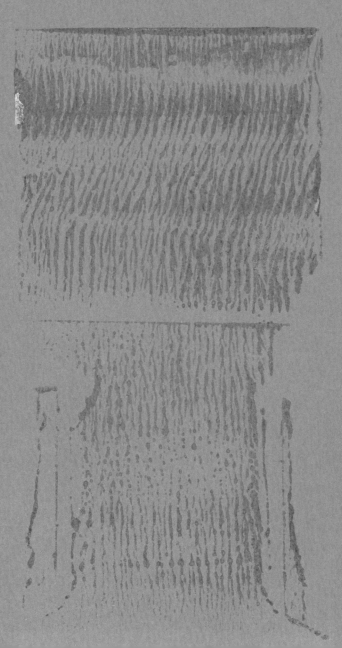